Cave Notes

First Reflections on Sense and Spirit

ROBERT E. MEAGHER

FORTRESS PRESS
Philadelphia

Dedicated, on my feet,
to the fond memory of

Frank O'Malley

once and future
founder and rector of
Christ College

Raba said:
How stupid people are, who stand before a Torah Scroll and do not stand up before a great man!
Makkot 22a

Library of Congress Catalog Card Number 75–13041

ISBN 0–8006–0430–X

5108G75 Printed in U.S.A. 1–430

ACKNOWLEDGMENTS

This slim work is a brief chronicle of paths pursued and to be pursued, a journal of maps and notes to which I have endeavored to give some provisional coherence. It is a work neither of solitude nor of resolution. I think and learn best in the midst of conversations and arguments which are mostly unresolved and unremittingly many-sided. Thus it would be dreadfully tedious, though warranted, for me to list those from whom I have learned most, only then to be obliged to confess the inadequacies and distortions in my learning. Perhaps justice lies in sheer silence, confident that others will see where they have led me and overlook where I have eluded their best efforts at setting me right.

However, there are two persons who, for quite different reasons, never entered into the discussions responsible for this book and yet to whom I remain deeply indebted for the very conditions which make an effort of this kind possible. The first is the late Frank O'Malley, the once and future founder of Christ College, within whose wall-less precincts my most faithful efforts aspire to occur and abide. A preeminent teacher of teachers, Mr. O'Malley, in his own words, wished to lead others to grasp the truth "tasted with the mind and thought with the fingers." His memory questions and sustains and illumines my own quest for sense and spirit. And then there is Susan Blakiston, whose extraordinary wit and hospitality have humored and housed my writing in an inimitable and unforgettable fashion.

R.E.M.

Anelog, Aberdaron
Caernarvonshire
Summer 1974

CONTENTS

> The task of the modern educator is not to cut down jungles but to irrigate deserts.
>
> C. S. Lewis

PROLOGUE

EDUCATING

If I were compelled to name with a single word the central and abiding concern of this book, I should say simply "education": a most serious and inescapable work. I find myself teaching, and being taught, with nearly every waking hour, whether spent among students or family or friends or alone. Education, as its name suggests, is a drawing forth of the merely possible into the fullness of the actual, an evoking of our fullest energies from the sleep and the forgetfulness wherein they and we lie concealed and unrealized. Mostly we live like bats in soulless, soundless caves, fleeing the light of day, slung upside down, clinging to the solid comfort of our rock-fast certainties, few, but ours and familiar. Education is a matter of flinging others into the sharp and shadowed light of day and of allowing ourselves to be flung there. As such it is a violent and painful process, as any birth appears to be. Man is, as the Greeks would say, thrown up, sprung, of the earth, made to stand erect, poised, balanced between sky and soil, between what crawls upon the ground and what turns in the heavens. Man must be reared into his proper life between the earth and the sun. Education is a matter of laying hold upon that life and of living it more abundantly. I fear that I, that we, live far removed from this abundance and that our thirst and hunger and deprivation are great. We have much to learn from others who have lived more closely and faithfully to their simplest possibilities, and among these the Indians who could describe themselves and their education in words such as these:

> These people's fathers were not without instruction.
> The earth was their teacher.
> The earth is the true teacher.

That is where the Indian first discovered
    that he was a human being.
And the earth taught you in the same way.
From that you found out
    how the earth was.
That is why we talk to each other
    with our bodies
    with friendly feelings.
Both were made from the same ground.[1]

We do ourselves no service when we delude ourselves with claims to pure matter or to pure spirit. As men, dust blown up and into life, we know nothing directly of either the utterly material or the utterly spiritual. We are as incapable of pure thought as we are of purely mechanized response. Both are mere hypotheses, the dreams of would-be angels and of would-be stones, usually so down-to-earth and so vocal that they complicate and belie their own claims before the day is out. There can be no education, no discovery of and sharing in our fullest possibilities as men and women, without our bodies, their manners and expressions and feelings, nor without friendly feelings. Education, then, can hardly be well-suited to self-indulgent youth camps where bodies sit and souls flit and friendly feelings are left for more private times and places. Education is not a matter of schooling as we mostly understand it but a matter of *schōlē*, as the Greeks understood it, of leisure. I have experienced the writing of this book as a quite leisurely, friendly work and I will entrust its reading to friendly, leisured souls.

In the writing of the *Laws*, Plato is an old man concerned with the young and with right beginnings. He says that man seems a mild creature "wont to prove more god-like and gentle than any other if he have but the right natural endowments and the right schooling," and yet "let him be trained insufficiently or amiss and he will show himself more savage than anything on the face of the earth."[2] Clearly, this training, if it is to be appropriate and conducive to man's finer possibilities, must not only involve but also be centered in an informed, critical, and passionate vision of what is true and good and right. Education within a democratic, pluralistic society such as ours is not relieved of ethical and religious questions and concerns; rather it is driven with sheer urgency to confront such questions and concerns without the limits, assurances, and prejudice of established dogmas and codes. Education is unavoidably ethical and religious. Its task is to rear men and women who delight in the fullness of their lives, workers who take pride in the quality of their work, and citizens who bear responsibility for the integrity of their actions. The avoidances of modern pluralistic education, embarrassed and shy of spiritual traditions and skills, have abandoned us to the genius of the profane and perverse.

Thus I cannot accept the idea that our proper schooling lies in the urbane skills of making conversation and making a living, each in his own preferred style and time. Rather, the skills we require most are the skills of mortality—the soul and the spittle to accept and to share, decently, even nobly, even more graciously, a common human calling and a common human fate. The proper aim of education is then, above all else, not competence but wisdom, which has always been seen to be at one with holiness. It is fitting that education should undertake the discipline demanded for the full and decent living of one's life and dying of one's death. This wisdom and holiness and their attending discipline are not the preserve or the preoccupation of a single generation or time of life or period of history. They are the concern of the young when one is young and the concern of the old when one is old. And they are the proper and common concern of all, young and old, dead and dying, and not yet born. We rear, we educate one another into our shared being; we call one another into our common and respective callings. There is nothing private or intimate about education properly understood. Its circle is open; its fabric without seams. In part, then, education demands that the young converse with the old, and that the living converse with the dead. In fact, education may be said to be one's "coming of age" among the living and among the dead.

"From infancy I came to boyhood, or rather it came to me, taking the place of infancy. Yet infancy did not go: for where was it to go to? Simply it was no longer there. For now I was not an infant, without speech, but a boy speaking."[3] With these few words, simple and telling and wondrous, Saint Augustine marks his coming of age as a child. Much the same might be thought and spoken of the other human ages from the time of their approaching or from the time of their passing. Where is my middle age and where my old age and how is it that they await me? Am I a child dreaming the dream of age or am I aged dreaming the dream of a child or am I ageless dreaming the dreams of youth and age? Or are those dreams perchance dreaming me?

Beginnings and endings and middles, youth and age, weave a single fabric—in the family, in the city, in the individual life—in loving and thinking and speaking and acting and hating. There are never sheer beginnings nor sheer endings; nothing is ever simply new or simply old or simply midstream. We look and speak and share over and across our pasts and futures, between lives and within a world that are always newborn and decadent and tired of themselves and dancing. Each person is always inevitably coming of age as a child or as a youth or as one in the full grasp of one's powers or as weakened in their loss. We circle these rings, tracing their stories as we grow and flower and lean brittle; and as we do so we seek insight and recognition—together. Machiavelli once said that only to valleys is it given to see hills and only to heights is it given to see valleys. He then goes on to suggest that it is the common man who is stationed so as to know well the nature of princes and the prince whose station permits him to see rightly the nature of the common man. Perhaps the same might be said of the human ages. Perhaps youth is the worst judge of itself, and so with age and maturity. Perhaps, too, the ancients were often their own worst judges and we ours. If so, we may hope to learn and to grow as we converse with our forefathers. This book will seek out the beginnings of such conversations.

Perhaps every age must encounter human fate and human mystery each time appropriately masked, perhaps playfully—perhaps maliciously, so as to be both understood and mistaken, elusive and recurrent. And so the youth encounters mortality and limits as in prospect and struggles towards the acceptance implied in making promises, whereas the same mortality and the same limits appear later in retrospect, requiring acceptance as forgiveness. The young man hates as if he will hate forever and loves as if he will love forever; while the old man, schooled in life's reversals to the impermanence of things and of one's own resolves, loves as if he will one day hate and hates as if he will one day love. And so, says Aristotle, the young love and hate too much and the old love and hate not enough. And so our lives are tangled in crossings over and back in which there is seldom a meeting or a consensus or a blessing.

Finally it is not a matter of tracing the ring of a single year, a single age, or even a single life. For I myself and we together and our common world know and speak of and celebrate birth and death, the seasons and the turnings of growth and decay, always all at once. Our dance somehow embraces the tree of both life and death, the tree of both good and evil—hand in hand—in a moment in which we might say with Augustine: "Every particle of sand in the glass of time is precious to me."[4] Some such moment might well be one's deepest and fondest hope from education. And yet its realization would be a sheer grace and not the fruit of this or any other effort at understanding or undertaking the work of education.

This present work will take up the discipline of education, the irrigation of what I know myself to be dry and unyielding to the plow. These reflections must sink deeply into our shared past and converse its renewing streams back into our lives. It will be a discipline of conversations in which we must strike the center of our lost and forgotten possibilities and disclose the historical and sensory origins of our most traditional and accessible wisdoms—the "Greek" wisdom which begins with wonder, the "Hebrew" wisdom which begins with the fear of the Lord, the "Roman" wisdom which begins with the founding, and the "modern" wisdom which begins with radical doubt. These traditions will be our conversants as we seek to come of age. Admittedly they will be "characterized," perhaps even caricatured, as we proceed. But what is a caricature unless a sketch all too true, overstated to assure recognition? Unless the past be characterized, given a mask, a persona, its voice will not reach our ears, or its face our eyes. At first our conversations and recognitions must know something of contrivance and single-mindedness. Its myriad faces and moods and meanings and truths will reach us in good time. William James offers an image in which we might see our present discipline when he says: "As the bees in swarming cling to one another in layers til the few are reached whose feet grapple the bough from which the swarm depends: so with the objects of our thinking,—they hang to each other by associated links, but the *original* source in all of them is the native interest which the earliest one once possessed."[5] It is this "native interest" which we hope to discern and to regain and which alone will direct and sustain our efforts to educate ourselves and others, to lead one another into the full light of our possibilities and into the full possession of our human being. I suspect that what Hippocrates says of the discipline of medicine is true, even more so, of the discipline of education: "Life is short, the art is long, opportunity fleeting, experiment dangerous, and judgement difficult."[6] Such words humble rather than excuse this beginning and what follows.

NOTES

1. Quoted from the Ward-Phillips lectures given by William Arrowsmith at the University of Notre Dame, March 6–9, 1972.

2. Plato *Laws* 6. 766a, trans. A. E. Taylor, in *Plato: The Collected Dialogues*, Bollingen Series, no. 71 (New York: Pantheon Books, 1966).

3. Augustine *Confessions* 1. 2., trans. F. W. Sheed (New York: Sheed & Ward, 1942).

4. Augustine *Confessions* 11. 2., trans. R. S. Pine-Coffin (Baltimore: Penguin Books, 1961).

5. William James, *Talks to Teachers on Psychology and to Students on Some of Life's Ideals* (New York and London: Henry Holt & Co., 1899), p. 99.

6. Cf. Hippocratic *Aphorisms* 1. 1., cited in Werner Jaeger, *Paideia: The Ideals of Greek Culture*, trans. Gilbert Highet (New York: Oxford University Press, 1944), 3:20.

Man's thinking is his soul's trek abroad.
Hippocrates

CHAPTER ONE

IMAGING

We begin abroad, with another's words and with another's thoughts. "A man's work is nothing," wrote Albert Camus, "but this slow trek to rediscover, through the detours of art, those two or three great and simple images in whose presence his heart first opened."[1] Nature, the earth, whatever man has never designed nor constructed, appears to develop towards the always more complex; while man, the most complex of the earth's creatures, reaches towards what is simple and one, or is at least only several. We describe now a circle, a circuit man walks with his thoughts which emerge intimately from his pores as perspiration on a journeyman's back or as mist on a morning's stream. A man's true thoughts are as close and dear to him as are his feet. They get him around. They lift him into the light of day. They tell him when he has reached day's end and done a day's work. They are without pretense.

Often our thinking is indeed a "slow trek," and yet this seems far too tame an image for thoughts often thickened with violence, for thoughts prepared to drive us mad. Plato's image of the mind as an aviary[2] crammed with countless untrained birds suggests some of the frenzy of thinking which would then be one's reaching in to seize the bird of choice in the midst of winged, screeching chaos. I myself prefer a still more violent image for thinking, the image of one who sets out to seize an enchanter. There are stories of enchanters[3] who, when seized and throttled ever so tightly by a pursuer, would change themselves into every manner of beast and frightful creature from dragons to mountain streams. And yet, as the legends go, if the pursuer never lost heart and even for an instant relaxed his grip, the enchanter would despairingly return to his original form and grant any single wish his pursuer's heart desired. Most pursuers themselves despaired along the way, yielding to the enchanter's dreadful power and occasionally to his cleverness. Thus many were cindered by dragon's fire, drowned astride a whale's back, or seduced by and wedded to a lover's charms. In fact, I know of no accounts of those who did not perish, no such accounts which have the ring of truth to them. Perhaps we have here a suitable image for the illusive and violent resistance of truth which we can think only in images which either slip away or deaden us into dogmatism which, as Lessing assures us, is merely the point at which we have tired of thinking. And yet this image of the pursuit of an enchanter through his myriad, marvelous metamorphoses is itself quite wanting in that it always describes single pursuits, one man's thoughts from birth to death. It is locked within single life-stories and gives no account of history.

We have now before us in mind two images for thinking: that of a slow trek backwards or homewards and that of a harrowing series of trials upon an enchanter's back in pursuit of one's heart's desire. With the addition of a single further image we shall have our "two or three great and simple images" from which this work of thought will unfold and towards which it will work its way back. It is my hope that in the presence of these images our hearts will open, troubled and desirous, questioned and questioning. It is my hope that these few images will provide our reflections with a center to think from and to drive towards, a whirling center drawing us back to it and to ourselves while flinging us out into the dark otherness abroad. It is my hope that there is energy, possibility and power, in these images that will sustain us and leave us weary.

My final image is that of the theater, ideally the theater of Aeschylus. Of the known Greek classical playwrights, Aeschylus may be said to have had the most immediate and the grandest sense of the theater. He reared his plays himself from conception to costumes to choreography. And, unlike Sophocles and Euripides, he twice employed a full trilogy of plays to unfold a single *mythos* or plot, once the plot of Prometheus and once the plot of Orestes. It is the *Oresteia*, and particularly the *Agamemnon*, in which Aeschylus' conception and mastery of the theater as metaphor reaches its fullest expression, and it is there that we will focus our sustained reflections in search of a last and master image.

As any classical play is concerned to do, the *Agamemnon* presents a *drama*, a deed—in this instance the murder of King Agamemnon by Clytaemnestra, his wife and queen. And yet it does not present this *drama* isolated from other deeds, as a thread pulled loose from a fabric of deeds past and future. Rather, the central *drama* is set against an appropriate *skēnē* or scene which it shares with other deeds and is spun in weblike fashion within its own *mythos* or narrative context. There is a story, a narrative past and future, within every deed. The sword-thrust which fells Agamemnon does not truly visit the city of Mycenae as a lightning-flash clean of human precedent and consequence. It is an act of murder, a human deed. And to tell of human deeds is to tell their stories, to reach into the past to find their origin and to penetrate the future as far as their outcome. But how far back and forth do human actions extend?

Most modern plays are played indoors, under artificial lighting. When the theater lights are cut, the theater and all in it are plunged into a darkness and a silence which break the continuity of conversations and concerns trailing in from outdoors and from each one's out-of-these-doors life. Theater and audience alike cease to be when and where and who they were and await those who will construe and fashion them afresh. Within the imaginative oblivion that is therein created, new lights illumine a new reality, fresh voices are heard, and fresh lives are possible. The modern theater is, then, most appropriately a place of creation.

Not so in the theater of Dionysus. In the classical Greek theater, the theater of Aeschylus, open to the sun as if spread out to ripen, there can be no artificial silence and darkness with which to end the old and begin the new. The day has its own brilliance and sounds in which theater and audience remain when and where and who they are. Even the plots are never new; rather, it is always a matter of coming to understand these plots and the people who stem from them, ever more deeply and fully. Scene, costume, and gesture are highly stylized; shadows are long and sharp in the day's sun. The lighting, the illumination of the *drama,* its meaning, its context, come from beyond the theater's own proper possibilities and the playwright's craft.

In the *Agamemnon*, it is the watchman's speech which draws the curtain and blocks out the lines of force which will have their way. These words first articulate the scene against which and the theater within which the *drama*, the murder of Agamemnon, will soon stand revealed. The watchman, in a dogged posture, is poised in darkness, confused and apprehensive, awaiting the light which is to come from afar. The awaited light is twofold: it is the dawn, the day's light which will bring to light and judgment the unfaithful sleep of the queen and her lover which the night permits and obscures; and it is the signal fire which will announce the end of a long war from which this city has long suffered. The first revelation is a matter of time; lucid day and the gaze of the city eventually come to bear upon every offense cloaked in private night. The second is a matter of fate and redemption. When the Greek fleet set sail for Troy, it was decreed that a signal flame should be beaconed from mountain peak to mountain peak and carried aloft across plains by swift runners until at last, in Clytaemnestra's words,

> Kindled once more with stintless heaping force, they send
> the beard of flame to hugeness, passing far beyond
> the promontory that gazes on the Saronic strait
> and flaming far, until it plunged at last to strike
> the steep rock of Arachnus near at hand, our watchtower.[4]

For now we should be sure to note that the "stage" lights come from afar to illumine the *drama* and to bring to crisis and clarity the fear of watchman and chorus. Both lights are beyond man; the sun rises of itself and the signal flame is merely handed on by human arrangement and craft, whereas we are told it was first lit by Hephaestus, the ugly and ill-tempered smith-god. Finally we might see both lights become one, a single metaphor, if we consider that "Hephaestus" may well derive from the words *hēmerophaistos* and thus mean "the one who shines by day." In any event we are in search of a master-image as we consider the light which brings the new day and history.

That light is but an image for the illumination of human *drama* is clear as we see that it is neither the dawn itself nor the manifest flames of a burning Troy which illuminate the *drama*, the deed, in question, the murder of Agamemnon. In fact both the dawn and the flames themselves exist only in image, in the imaginative speech of the theater. Rather it is the *logos*, the word, which calls the theater, the "seeing-place," into existence, that comes from afar to shine upon a deed, a people, and a time, bringing them to a clear and full unity. It is in the speeches that light floods in upon the *drama* dragging it from the obscure, dark privacy of the royal chambers to a common public place to be seen by all and understood by all. This full trek or *peripateia* is not complete until the establishment of the court of justice in *The Eumenides*. And yet we need not follow the descent of the word to the point of its institutionalization in order to grasp its power and meaning as image.

As the light of day and victory is unfurled from the place of the gods into the now of the theater, the now of the theater is imaginatively dilated to embrace the seemingly forgotten past and the seemingly unforeseeable future—not the past and the future simply, but, pointedly, the past and the future of the *drama*, the murderous deed. Deeds become living things with roots and fruit, progenitors and offspring, of their own, organisms with their own *physis*, or cycle of birth and growth and decay. That Clytaemnestra grasps the driving inner necessity of deeds once conceived and undertaken is evident from what she says of the moment when she struck down her king and husband:

> Thus he went down, and the life struggled out of him;
> and as he died he spattered me with the dark red
> and violent driven rain of bitter savored blood
> to make me glad, as gardens stand among the showers
> of God in glory at the birthtime of the buds.[5]

The imagery here is that of sheer Dionysiac and sexual frenzy which pours into so many of Clytaemnestra's words spoken in the orgasm of lucid action. She describes and embodies an ecstasy in which activity and passivity, freedom and necessity, flow into one and congeal even as they spill into one another. At the moment of orgasm the past and the future flood the present and we are overwhelmed, forgetful of parent and child, birth and death, forgetful perhaps by virtue of the immediacy rather than the distance of each. At this moment we are filled with a power in the presence and possession of which we are simply irresponsible and unanswerable. Only in the before and after where the past and future may enter and must enter do we become accountable and thus free. The central act of the *Agamemnon* is the murder of Agamemnon—one act embracing the action of Clytaemnestra and the passion of Agamemnon who become sexually and fatally one—as ecstasy and as drama. Clytaemnestra embodies the ecstasy; the watchman, the chorus, and Cassandra imaginatively expand that moment of ecstasy into drama.

The watchman, perched high above the city and peering into the dark night soon to become day, is far from the obscuring passion and sleep of the queen and her lover. He is poised, precariously and painfully, in a posture of tension. He speaks of and for a house dis-eased and out of joint, a house which "itself, could it take voice, might speak aloud and plain."[6] Finally, in his half-dread and half-hope, he says that he speaks to those who understand, which can only mean the citizens, not the chorus of Mycenae but the people of Athens who alone are witness to the drama and see fully the deed in the "seeing-place," the theater. And yet the chorus understands in part and responds to the watchman by reaching the present deed into the past or by reaching into the past of the present deed. Clytaemnestra is not the first to be unfaithful nor is Agamemnon the first to die a savage, unwarranted death. There are ample precedents in the house of Atreus for all that is now to be endured. There is the unfaithfulness of Helen whose promiscuous wedding was well attended by both sides for ten long years, by Agamemnon, for one, who now returns unabashedly beside his royal mistress, Cassandra. And long before either of these there was Agamemnon's grandmother who slept with her husband's (Atreus') brother (Thyestes). In return, Atreus laid before his brother a splendid banquet with Thyestes' children, well-disguised, as the main dish. Nor is Clytaemnestra without a past or precedent in promising a marriage bed while she sharpens a blade to be thrust home to her own advantage. For, ten years before her act, Agamemnon sent word to his own daughter, Iphigeneia, to garland herself to be wed to Achilles, while it was the priest Chalchas, not

Achilles, who prepared an altar, and not a bed, on which her virgin blood would spill for fair winds to Troy. Add to all of this the ravaging of Troy consummated in the murder of Cassandra. Incident upon incident, the full story of unfaithfulness and slaughter is recounted with a lyric intensity and a concentrated repetition of images that tells not of many deeds but of one deed, one story, one *drama.*

When the past has become imaginatively and dramatically present, which is to say, when the present emerges clearly as rooted and tangled in the past, the tale is only yet half told. For any isolated act has its outcome as well as its beginning, its consequences as well as its precedents. As an organism, actions are always both parent and child with ancestors and heirs of their own. We must now speak of the future, which is to say, we must listen to the words of Cassandra, cursed with prophesies to which no one attends ever. To Cassandra, "keen-scented like some hound upon the scent of blood,"[7] it is given to reveal the future, not the future simply but the future of the *drama*, the central deed of adulterous regicide. After assuring the chorus that they would surely look upon Agamemnon dead, Cassandra tells of her own death, the last victim of Troy, and of the unspeakable death of Clytaemnestra smitten in revenge by a viprous son born of her and banished. With a brain "whirling . . . in a storm of things foreseen"[8] and in a vision so despairingly total, Cassandra leaps from what has been to what shall be, from the murderous past to the murderous future; and the two become one. She cannot inhabit the brief security of the present in which the chorus blindly forgets and hopes; for she knows the wickedness in this house to be ancient like a forest deep-rooted, a source of endless violence no less than an outraged sea. "Now," says Cassandra:

> I will tell you plainly and from no cryptic speech;
> bear me then witness, running at my heels upon
> the scent of these old brutal things done long ago.
> There is a choir that sings as one, that shall not again
> leave this house ever; the song thereof breaks harsh with menace.
> And drugged to double fury on the wine of men's
> blood shed, there lurks forever here a drunken rout

> of ingrown vengeful spirits never to be cast forth.
> Hanging above the hall they chant their song of hate
> and the old sin; and taking up the strain in turn
> spit curses on that man who spoiled his brother's bed.
> Did I go wide, or hit, like a real archer? Am I
> some swindling seer who hawks his lies from door to door?
> Upon your oath, bear witness that I know by heart
> the legend of ancient wickedness within this house.[9]

Here too is ecstasy. Not the ecstasy of Clytaemnestra—powerful, effective, and irresponsible. Rather it is the ecstasy of the muse-driven poet, the ecstasy of the theater—weak, ineffectual, forgetful of nothing, mindful of *drama*, of human doing and human suffering. Signal fires, the rising dawn, and the vision of the seer converge as images of human imagination, that is of the capacity to see human action and passion, or to render it seeable, as a story within its full narrative context. Let us show forth now our most ranging thoughts regarding that context, the *skēnē* which Aeschylus as dramatic poet erects behind and from within the single deed in which Agamemnon and Clytaemnestra, action and passion, man and woman, living and dying, mingle confusedly. The imaginative dilation of human *drama* which is dramatic poetry represents, as we have said, an inquiry into the *physis* of human doing and suffering, and is thus, in the simplest and original sense, *historia*.[10] History as inquiry and art is rooted in the perception that a deed, to be understood and judged aright, must be unraveled and spread out imaginatively into the full light of day, namely into the imaginatively reconstructed past and future. The simple fact is that the murder of Agamemnon cannot be known or seen—it is decisively obscured and thus unintelligible—apart from a web of deeds ranging at least from the first unfaithfulness of the wife of Atreus to the acquittal of Orestes for his avenging matricide. The murder of Agamemnon is not a whole action or passion but a moment in a movement of growth and decay, a moment in the life and death of an organism. History and drama, as inquiry into *physis*, must begin with the beginning and reach to the ending; they must span the coming-to-be and the ceasing-to-be of any fact such as that the unfaithful queen has slain her king. Above all Aegisthus, son to

Thyestes and lover to Clytaemnestra, would have it otherwise. He, "sword-handed" and well-guarded, and Clytaemnestra, in what seems like her postorgasmic depression, would have it end with this mere fact that a queen has changed lovers and kings. But the doing and the suffering have not come to term. There is no hindering what must come of what has already been done and suffered. Otherwise there is only willful ignorance and forgetfulness, the self-delusion of those who would act with impunity and with innovation; and it is indeed with words ignorant and forgetful that Aegisthus closes the *Agamemnon* and leads his mistress into the obscuring privacy of their chambers: "forget them, dearest; you and I have the power."[11] They imagine themselves to be standing at the sheer origin of their deeds as well as at their term. In fact it is given to no one, neither king nor slave, neither slayer nor slain, to stand beyond and encompass one's doings and one's sufferings. In short, our intentions, what we have in mind as we act or as we endure, the way we would have both, are but dreams which spring from and haunt but hardly control the facts of our lives.

But we might step further and say that the individual life as action and passion, as *drama*, is simply unintelligible apart from the full imaginative context which encompasses it. Self-inquiry and self-understanding reach of necessity beyond *my* past and *my* future into *our* past and *our* future and towards *the* past and *the* future. In short, the individual life-story is not an intelligible whole either in the telling or in the living. To give a true account of any *drama*, to give an account of one's life, to live and to tell one's life as story requires that one discover and disclose its own coming-to-be and ceasing-to-be and thus requires that one give an account of human and even divine history, i.e., that one tell not only the stories of other men but that one tell the stories of the gods. Otherwise one lives and speaks of one's living without insight and understanding, privately and obscuredly. In Goethe's words:

> Wer nicht von dreitausend Jahren
> Sich weiss Rechenschaft zu geben,
> Bleib' im Dunkeln unerfahren,
> Mag von Tag zu Tage leben.[12]

[If a man can give no account to himself
of three thousand years,
Let him dwell in darkness, inexperienced
May he live from day to day.]

Amidst these perhaps circuitous reflections on the *Agamemnon* we may have glimpsed with some clarity and fullness the simple, telling power of this third and master-image for thinking, the image of the signal flame, kindled by the gods, and passed across the spaces and times of many lives to illumine the otherwise isolated *drama* of Agamemnon's destruction. The stories of the gods initiate and encompass the stories of men in the midst of which the stories of any given single lives unfold. Life-stories require to be illumined by human history and human history requires to be illumined by myth. This insight is neither peculiarly germane nor acceptable to modern sensitivity whose contrary cosmology may be perceived in Sartre's account of the cosmos within which he tells the story of his own life in *The Words*:

> I was the beginning, middle and end gathered together in a tiny little boy already old, already dead, *here*, in the shadow . . . and *outside*, far far away, in the great dismal sun of glory. I was the corpuscle at the beginning of its trajectory and the train of waves that flows back on it after crashing into the buffer. Boxed in, pulled together, touching my tomb with one hand and my cradle with the other, I felt brief and splendid, a flash of lightning that was blotted out by darkness.[13]

We have here a clear reversal of images in which it is the unique and solitary life which alone, though with brief futility, illumines the dark unintelligible otherness abroad which is experienced as and presumed to be a threatening nothingness. As we shall see more fully in the course of our reflections, Sartre's vision is altogether characteristic of the modern abridged imagination. And yet, despite the hard and fast closure of this vision, in fact, deep within it, there is a restless, haunting curiosity regarding the encompassing otherness as a possible source of illumination and meaning. This curiosity finds splendid expression in the guileless, earnest, and quite comically misdirected inquiry of Lenny in Pinter's *The Homecoming*:

LENNY: I'll tell you what, Dad, since you're in the mood for a bit of a . . . chat, I'll ask you a question. It's a question I've been meaning to ask you for some time. That night . . . you know . . . the night you got me . . . that night with Mum, what was it like? Eh? When I was just a glint in your eye. What was it like? What was the background to it? I mean, I want to know the real facts about my background. I mean, for instance, is it a fact that you had me in mind all the time, or is it a fact that I was the last thing you had in mind? [Pause] I'm only asking this in a spirit of inquiry, you understand that, don't you? I'm curious. And there's lots of people of my age share that curiosity, you know that, Dad? They often ruminate, sometimes singly, sometimes in groups, about the true facts of that particular night—the night they were made in the image of those two people *at it*. It's a question long overdue, from my point of view, but as we happen to be passing the time of day here tonight I thought I'd pop it to you.[14]

However estranged the telling and the living of life-stories may now be from history and from myth, we have only to look beyond the secular cloister of modern thinking to find the assumed convergence of the three. When Augustine, in his *Soliloquies*, holds a conversation with his own reason, there occurs this early and critical exchange:

REASON: What then do you wish to know?
AUGUSTINE: All that I have mentioned in my prayer.
REASON: Briefly summarize it.
AUGUSTINE: I desire to know God and the soul.
REASON: Nothing more?
AUGUSTINE: Nothing whatever.
REASON: Begin your quest, then.[15]

The search for the soul and the search for God are, as Augustine comes to know both, a single quest—at one time an inquiry into his own Christian life and at another time an inquiry into the life of the Christian church, and at still another time an inquiry into the trinitarian life of the Christian God. The proper order of his questioning is clear from two quite brief sections from his *Confessions*:

And I turned to myself and said:
"And you, who are you?"
And I answered: "A man."

> What then am I, O my God? What
> nature am I?[16]

Augustine is unable to know *who* he is, unable to tell his own life-story, until he is able to know *what* he is, able to tell the story of man. And yet to know man he must know God of whom man is but an image. His quest is one of recollection; and, for Augustine, the memory of man is at once the memory of one's own past, the memory of the human past and, finally, the memory of the eternal. What "is true of a man's whole life, of which all his actions are parts . . . is true of the whole history of mankind of which each man's life is a part."[17] And finally what is true of man is also true of God. It is not a flaw but a peculiar fullness of vision that accounts for the fact that the *Confessions*, in which Augustine tells his own story, works towards and ends with a series of meditations upon the Book of Genesis. We see here the now familiar course from the story of one's self to the story of one's history to the story of one's god, from personal to shared to sacred history.

Similarly, in quite different soil and within our own near past, there is the account which the eminent Apache warrior Geronimo has given of his own life. His story begins in *the* beginning with the Apache myth of origins when the world was covered with darkness. He tells of the primordial war of the beasts and the eagles and of the emergent primacy of man. He tells of the boy Apache, taught by Usen (God), victorious over the horny-scaled dragon and founder of the Apache nation. He tells the history of the Apache Indians, tracing finally his own lineage, numbering and naming his own elder brothers and sisters. And only then does he begin to tell what we would call "his story" with these words:

> As a babe I rolled on the dirt floor of my father's tepee, hung in my tsoch at my mother's back, or suspended from the bough of a tree. I was warmed by the sun, rocked by the winds, and sheltered by the trees as other Indian babes.
>
> When a child my mother taught me the legends of our people; taught me of the sun and sky, the moon and stars, the clouds and storms. She also taught me to kneel and pray to Usen for strength, health, wisdom, and protection. . . .

> My father had often told me of the brave deeds of our warriors, of the pleasures of the chase, and the glories of the warpath.[18]

The slow trek homewards, the violent metamorphoses of the enchanter, the signal flame lit and relit and passed down through many hands—all of these images speak of process and multiplicity, of the myriad, moving incarnations of thought. They preclude any thinking and speaking that would disclaim, or seek to strip itself of, metaphor. *Legein*, thinking and speaking (quite appropriately the same word in Greek), reflects and shares in the brilliance of the real and the true as any shining surface somehow retains and participates in the sun. Nonetheless, the grasp of thinking and speaking upon the true is loose and fleeting. The truth of any word or image perishes. Men would do well to imagine themselves thinking and speaking always at ocean's edge. They construct their words and thoughts as structures in the sand, with some stature and cohesion; and yet the sea must always come to wash away their thoughts, not that they were altogether false or illusory but rather that they belong to time and must be thought through and spoken each time afresh.

To think upon thinking is to reflect upon metaphor, that is to reflect upon participatory degrees of reality and truth. In metaphor there is always a relationship between image and original. Consider how the willow is reflected in the pond. The willow rooted on shore is real and the willow to be seen in the pond is real, namely, both are real willows; but they are not equally real willows. The willow to be seen in the pond both is and is not a willow. When Pascal says that man is a reed, we are required to add that man both is and is not a reed. What we mean is that the sight in the pond resembles a willow and that man resembles a reed or, perhaps more precisely, that the sight in the pond may be seen as a willow and that man may be thought of as a reed. What is essential is the "both is and is not," the capacity of man to distinguish not merely between the real and the nonreal but as well between the less real and the more real, namely to distinguish between degrees of being, between image and original.

Let us suppose for the moment a world in which anything whatever either is or is not. In such a world there can be no thought or talk of images or of imagining. Man is man and not reed; reed is reed and not man. All beings are properly discrete and unique and must be assigned appropriately discrete and unique names. In this case, naming must mean the numbering of arbitrarily distinguished objects; and metaphor would represent confusion rather than depth of perception. Even so, there remains the necessity of communication which is simply impossible if all names are numbers and if you and I begin, as we would, in different places with different objects in assigning 1, 2, 3, etc. Even in a world so conceived there must be communication just as there must be commerce; and words may be thought to function as a commonly accepted currency, as money of sorts. Money functions to relate essentially unrelated objects and activities; "it exchanges every quality and object for every other," explains Karl Marx, "even though they are contradictory. It is the fraternization of incompatibles; it forces contraries to embrace."[19] Thus, due to the phenomenon of money ("the galvano—*chemical* power of society —the bond of all *bonds*"[20]) the shining of a pair of shoes, two roasted pretzels, and a subway ride across the city are all equivalent, in worth. They all come to the same thing. Money does not represent nor disclose any essential relatedness or in-commonness among things but only established functional equivalences which permit men to do business with one another. Money brings together the butcher, the baker, and the candlestick maker, not through the disclosure of their common, though perhaps unequal, sharing in one being or truth, or good, but rather through the creation of an artificially common substance which Marx calls the "object par excellence"[21] and in terms of which they come to see their own proper activities, desires, needs, and aspirations. Thus money is the power to bring together and somehow relate what seems quite disparate; but it is also "the power to confuse and invert all human and natural qualities, to bring about fraternization of incompatibles . . . the universal whore, the universal pander among men."[22] As such, money "appears as a disruptive power for the individual and for the social bonds."[23]

It is no mere coincidence that money and dictionaries came into their own at approximately the same time in the West. For the modern conception of language, epitomized in the primacy of usage and thus of dictionaries of usage, bears remarkable resemblances to the modern conception of money. Throughout this brief account of language as conceptual currency I have had closely in mind the section "Of Speech" in the *Leviathan* of Thomas Hobbes for whom metaphor is an "abuse of speech" and for whom "in right definition lies the first use of speech."[24] It might illumine this discussion of money and language if we were simply to place one after the other what Marx says of money and what Hobbes says of language as powers prone to confusion and distortion:

> [Marx:] It [money] changes fidelity into infidelity, love into hate, hate into love, virtue into vice, vice into virtue, servant into master, stupidity into intelligence and intelligence into stupidity.[25]

> [Hobbes:] . . . For one man calleth *wisdom*, what another calleth *fear*; and one *cruelty*, what another *justice*; one *prodigality*, what another *magnanimity*; and one *gravity*, what another *stupidity*, etc.[26]

So long as one is preoccupied with the necessity and certainty of communication, one must be correspondingly preoccupied with "right," i.e., already agreed upon, definition. What such a conception of language overlooks or denies is the possibility of communion as disclosure and experience. So long as one asssumes, with Hobbes, that there is nothing in the world universal, namely, shared and common, but names,[27] then language can do nothing more or other than accidentally relate the essentially unrelated with a view towards certain necessary forms of shared discourse or commerce, in which case men continue to inhabit distinct worlds, although they come to share a common language. For Hobbes it is nonsense to speak of the soil, a horse, and a child as all three "thirsty," much less to speak at the same time of a man's "thirst" for justice or for revenge. And this would indeed be nonsense if we were not able to see how all of these thirsts have something truly in common. The common word discloses a common reality, and the glimpsed unity of somehow distinct, somehow common, realities becomes a genuine experience of communion. When we know a special joy and, at the sight of a bird, say that our heart too soars, we either speak out of a deep confusion, as Hobbes would claim, or we express an experienced in-commonness with that bird in flight, a common sharing in a world that is gracious and abounding. We may say it is a matter of choice but this is not to say that both choices possess the same validity.

Language and metaphor as the experience and expression of participation and communion live and breathe in the space between what simply is and what simply is not, the realm of becoming. This too is the proper sphere of the imagination as distinct from logic and metaphysics and of man as distinct from beasts and gods. For an animal, only hard and fast literal reality matters and an animal is thus simply incapable of dwelling, even for a moment, in the space between what exists and what does not. If a bird were to see the reflection of another bird in a pond it might leap into the pond for fellowship's sake. The reflection would be one moment bird and the next moment water (which is simply not—bird); never would it be for the bird what it is for man, the reflection of a bird. The reflection, the image, both is and is not a bird; and, as such, it is real. An animal is quite capable of seeing an image but not as image. Leonardo da Vinci speaks of household pets being deceived by paintings of their masters which they take to be in fact their masters. But this is not precisely the case. A dog may look at an image of his master and see his master. Then, perhaps after licking or sniffing the canvas, the dog looks at the image and sees something other than its master, something *not* his master. But the dog simply cannot look at the image as image. This imaging capacity, which Plato calls *eikasia* (from the word for image, *eikōn*) is peculiar to man. Man alone is an imaging being, capable of creating and of delighting in images, namely, in things which both are and are not.

Man's capacity for images is essentially related to his capacity for self-consciousness. For man is himself an image in that he always both is and is not. Man dwells in becoming. And thus when we notice that man is able to see images as images what we finally notice is that man is able to see himself, as image, as both being and not being what he is to be. Man is that peculiar being whose own coming and ceasing to be is of direct, conscious, thematic concern to him. This concern takes many forms and has many meanings; and we can do no more here than explore a few, quite simple, implications of man's being an image with a capacity to experience and know himself as image. What I am calling imaging (or *eikasia*) Augustine called memory (or *memoria*), of which he wrote:

> Great is the power of memory,
> a thing, o my God, to be in awe of,
> a profound and immeasurable multiplicity;
> and this thing is my mind, this thing
> am I. A life powerfully various
> and manifold and immeasurable.[28]

There is surely no one who is not minimally conscious of and concerned with his own becoming, namely, with himself as image. To encounter oneself as becoming, as dwelling in the space between what simply is and simply is not, is to encounter multiplicity and possibility. As I reflect in prospect upon who it is I shall be or upon what it is I shall do, I must consider a range of possibilities as multiple and various as my patience and imagination allow. In one sense, I *am* all that I am able to consider myself as one day being; and I *am doing* all that I am able to consider myself as doing. It is no matter that these possibilities conflict the one with the other. And yet, in another sense I am and do none of these things. The same might be said of the past as I consider all that I might have been or done. Surely I am somehow all that I might have been and done but failed to be and do, just as I am somehow none of them. Becoming is a conversation of the one with the many and of the many with the one, of being with nonbeing and of nonbeing with being. Most often we conceive of becoming as individuation or as becoming someone in particular. Becoming as individuation is a relentless movement from the many to the one, from the possibly many to the actually one. It is a process of literal exclusion: I must always do this and not that or that and not this. At any given moment I am always thinking or doing or suffering only one thing. If this is true, then it would seem to follow that I am always becoming someone in particular, someone quite unique, inevitably one and not many. And there surely is a certain literal truth to this process of individuation. But it is also true that at any given moment I am able to entertain myriad "past" possibilities I might have embraced and at least as many "future" possibilities I might still embrace; and at such a moment I am somehow all of them. Becoming, then, also involves a movement from the one to the many; and it is this latter movement which is of special interest to our present discussion. At any moment, to bring our thoughts briefly together, at any given moment, I am always only who I have been and who I shall be and yet I am not merely that. Also, I am somehow all those things which I am able to see myself as being and as having been, and yet not quite. Both require imagination to be both true and false. I am both the one self I am becoming and the many selves I shall never become. In the words of the Latin playwright Terence: *"Homo sum: humane nil a me alienum puto"* (I am a man and I see nothing human as unrelated to me).[29]

"I am a man." These few simple words may lead us a long way in our reflections. They recall Augustine's question, "Who am I?" and its response, "A man." The I, the self, the one person I am in the process of becoming, remains a man, not man simply, but *a* man. To say that I am a man is to say both that I am man and that I am not man, namely, to say that I am an image of man, man caught in the space between being and not being, caught in time, the changing image of eternity. The I, the self, becomes itself of necessity; the self is driven out of the many into the unique with all of the silent, unyielding effectiveness of the flaming swords once waved by the banishing angels of Eden. And yet the man, the fullness of the human, is never wholly *alienum*, never altogether lost to the individual self. I am a man and nothing human is ever finally lost to me. However forgetful or unmindful the self might be of what it means to be human, the self retains the capacity for remembering, for bringing to mind the full depth and scope of its humanity.

Again, this capacity for mindfulness, for bringing to mind the full drama of one's existence, is what we have called "imaging." Every image, however simple, leads from the one to the many, from the unique to the shared. When a primitive man paints a stag on the wall of his dwelling, that stag both is and is not the stag he has just seen, or tracked, or skinned. It is also every stag he has ever seen or will ever see and, for that matter, every stag you and I have ever seen or shall ever see. In simplest and yet telling expression, it is a stag. Imaging is each man's capacity to grasp and to share his humanity and his work. Imaging is each man's capacity to tell the stories of his deeds, to listen to and to tell the stories of other men's deeds, and, finally, the capacity to listen to and to tell the stories of the gods. Imaging is each one's capacity for theater, to act and to suffer revealed to others and to one's self just as others stand revealed in their deeds. Imaging is each man's profound delight and pain at the sight of his own diminished humanity recognized by and recognizably one with the many and diverse, yet still diminished, humanity of others.

Each human being or, more appropriately, each human becoming is always indefinably more and other than it shall ever see itself to be. Each self is both fact and possibility. And yet how is the self, in its own hard and fast literalness, to discover and call forth into some kind of being that indefinably more and other which it already somehow is? The self as a rule proceeds through life as an auto on a dark night's road, casting its slim path ahead of it as it quite literally makes its way it knows not where. As any one deed or life becomes more probable than any other, possibilities perish before one's eyes. And yet as long as any possible deed or life remains as probable or as improbable as any other, then one has no life of one's own, one is indeed no one in particular, and one might even lose one's proper name after some time and be known by a generic name such as "stranger" or "him." No, one must and is mostly inclined to follow the deadly clear path on which an identity and a name of one's own is to be achieved. And yet how does one illuminate the seemingly lost possibilities which he always somehow remains at least related to? The dark human otherness outside of the concerns and the ken of each self must reveal itself and be understood as it is revealed; and that revelation we call history.

History, says Martin Heidegger, is "the 'recurrence' of the possible."[30] History is the myriad traces men have consciously left and leave of themselves. In the broadest possible sense of "story," which would embrace tombs and walls and songs and carvings as well as writings, history is the stories men tell of and with their lives; it is the theater each man creates and visits so that he and others both somehow like and somehow unlike himself might stand revealed to themselves and to each other. History is the presence and the accessibility of the human other to each self, the human other which finally is seen not to be other (*alienum*). History represents for each self that indefinably more and other which it already somehow is and yet has never seen itself to be. History is the full spectrum of the human which the individual, in mindful moments, recollects and reflects and to which it cannot but contribute itself. Each time the self confronts the human other imaged for it in another's words or tears or gestures or works the self is called forth into a fuller humanity in which it sees itself somewhat less diminished and obscured. Each time two selves communicate and commune across a table or across three thousand years they become more than they knew themselves to be and other than they saw themselves to be. They are less inexperienced and less truly do they live in darkness from day to day.

And yet neither history nor memory may be appropriately confined to the past; for there seems to be truth in the words of Nietzsche's Zarathustra when he says that "some souls one will never discover, unless one invents them first."[31] These words return us, as we must return, to the truth, although partial, that each one must pass from the many to the one, from the many selves one might become to the one self one must become. There is some sure truth to the fact that man is born each time anew and that each man must do his own dying. And the uniqueness and the solitude of one's birth and death must reveal a dimension of fresh freedom in the course of what must come to pass from birth to death. Human coming-to-be as the encounter with history, the human other, ought not to obscure human coming-to-be as the encounter with self, the personal identity. Man as image, as always being and not being, always becoming, is properly engaged both in appropriation—the discovery of something shared—and in individuation—the creation of something unique.

One is able to avoid appropriation and live from day to day; and yet no one, living from day to day, is able to avoid individuation. No one is able to do or think or say more than one thing at a time, and I shall always be the one who thought this and not that and did that and not this. No one can do otherwise than become someone in particular. And yet, in this inevitable process of the exclusion of possibilities, can one know what one is doing in embracing one possibility and in excluding others? Can we speak of truth, beauty, goodness, faithfulness with respect to individuation? Has anyone ever claimed to know what he is doing in becoming the someone he is coming-to-be and in leading the life he comes to lead? For this to be a question at all one must experience the manyness and the variousness of the humanly possible, which is to say that one must encounter history; and the broader and deeper that encounter, the more urgent and endless this question becomes. Let us assume this question, the profound questionableness of our lives lived from day to day; and let us inquire in the remaining chapters of this work into what it might mean to pass rightly from the many to the one, to know what one is doing in one's becoming. In our inquiry into what this, let us say "wisdom," could mean, we would do well to begin with and perhaps not reach far beyond what it has already come to mean, namely, with the history of this question.

From the outset I make two assumptions. First I assume with Socrates "that some of the opinions which people entertain should be respected and others should not."[32] For, as he says, "serious thinkers . . . have always held some such view."[33] Thinking would be indeed a curious activity if one were able to weigh neither others' thoughts nor one's own. But so would living, or any seriousness with respect to living, be indeed curious if one were unable to weigh one's possibilities. The "possible" which recurs in history in all its multiplicity represents a vast array of opinions with respect to right doing and thinking and speaking. And surely "serious doers" have always held that some deeds, some lives, deserve more respect than others. Secondly I assume, with Deianeira, "that one should never plunge eagerly into anything obscure."[34]

NOTES

1. Albert Camus, *Lyrical and Critical Essays* (New York, Vintage, 1968), p. 17.

2. See Plato *Theaetetus* 197e–198b. Plato's own use of this image does not explicitly suggest this feathered chaos which would surely accompany the pursuit, seizure, and release of one bird after another in the aviary of the mind. And yet all this seems to be quite clearly implied in this image which is surely veined with irony and humor.

3. One such tale is that of the Old Man of the Sea in Homer *Odyssey* 4. 450ff.

4. Aeschylus *Agamemnon* trans. Richard Lattimore (Chicago: University of Chicago Press, 1953), ll. 30–59.

5. Ibid., ll. 1388–92.

6. Ibid., ll. 36–37.

7. Ibid., ll. 1093–94.

8. Ibid., l. 1216.

9. Ibid., ll. 1183–97.

10. Thucydides, for one, as historian and thus as narrative poet, is equally concerned to disclose and illumine the *physis*, the peculiar coming-to-be and ceasing-to-be, of human action and passion. The essential character of the Greek inquiry into *physis*, beginning it seems in medical speculation and pervading Greek thinking, will be discussed at length at a later point in our inquiry. See pp. 102–6.

11. Aeschylus, ll. 1673–75.

12. Cf. Hans Jonas, "Change and Permanence: On the Possibility of Understanding History," *Social Research* 38 (Autumn 1971), p. 526.

13. Jean-Paul Sartre, *The Words* (New York: Fawcett World Library, 1964), p. 153.

14. Harold Pinter, *The Homecoming* (New York: Grove Press, 1965), p. 36.

15. Augustine *The Soliloquies* 1. 2. 7, in *Augustine: Earlier Writings*, trans. John H. S. Burleigh (Philadelphia: Westminster Press, 1953), pp. 26–27.

16. Augustine *Confessions* 10.6 and 10.17, trans. F. W. Sheed (New York: Sheed & Ward, 1942), pp. 177, 186.

17. Augustine *Confessions* 11. 28, trans. R. S. Pine-Coffin (Baltimore: Penguin Books, 1961), p. 278.

18. Geronimo, *Geronimo: His Own Story,* ed. S. M. Barrett (New York: E. P. Dutton & Co., 1970), pp. 70–71.

19. Karl Marx, *Early Writings*, trans. T. B. Bottomore (New York: McGraw-Hill Book Co., 1963), p. 193.

20. Ibid., pp. 191, 192.

21. Ibid., p. 189.

22. Ibid., p. 198.

23. Ibid., p. 193.

24. Thomas Hobbes, *Leviathan* (New York: Crowell-Collier, 1962), p. 37.

25. Marx, p. 193.

26. Hobbes, p. 40.

27. See ibid., p. 35.

28. Augustine *Confessions* 10. 17 (trans. F. W. Sheed), p. 186.

29. Publius Terentius Afer *Heauton Timorumenos* 1. 25, Loeb Classical Library no. 22 (Cambridge, Mass.: Harvard University Press, 1912).

30. Martin Heidegger, *Being and Time*, trans. John Macquarrie and Edward Robinson (New York: Harper & Row, 1962), p. 444.

31. Friedrich Nietzsche, *Thus Spake Zarathustra*, in *The Portable Nietzsche*, trans. Walter Kaufmann (New York: Viking Press, 1954), p. 154.

32. Plato *Crito* 46c, trans. Hugh Tredennick (Baltimore: Penguin Books, 1914), p. 85.

33. Ibid.

34. Sophocles *The Women of Trachis* 2. 670–71, trans. Michael Jameson (Chicago: University of Chicago Press, 1957).

Alone I confront a tremendous problem. It is a forest in which I lose myself, a virgin forest. I need help. I need disciples. I need a master. To obey would be sweet. If I had lost myself on a mountain, I would obey the man who knew the mountain, and if I should meet a man capable of enlightening me on moral ideas, I would listen to him. But I find no one, no disciples and fewer masters. I am alone.

Friedrich Nietzsche

CHAPTER TWO

DECIDING

In our quest for wisdom, it would surely be in good order for us to begin formally where Augustine begins, with the question: "And you, who are you?"[1] In posing this question, Augustine says that he turns to himself and addresses this question to himself, whereas he addresses God and not himself when he inquires into his nature, into *what* he is. It is as if he were saying, with Bacon and perhaps even with Aristotle, that we can know, directly and immediately, only what we ourselves have fashioned and made. And, at least in a preliminary but real sense, we do fashion *who* we are. We do exercise some real control in that process of exclusion and choice in which we become *who* we are, always someone in particular. This is to say that we ordinarily have something in mind in doing this and not that, and as we suffer that and not this. Ordinarily our life unfolds before us not as "a tale told by an idiot, full of sound and fury, signifying nothing,"[2] but as a story with a beginning and an ending, with a plot and focus and concentration of energy, namely, as a meaningful whole often disquietingly ordered and orderly and thin. It is, then, part of the truth (not the whole truth) or the truth of a part (not the truth of the whole) to say that we tell the story of our lives. And yet, the individual life-story always occurs within a deeper and wider story, the story of one's times, the story of a shared time of life. The beginning and the ending of any single life is never a sheer beginning nor a sheer ending. No one ever simply begins his life afresh. Indeed, there is truth in the words of Qoheleth:

> What was will be again; what has been done will be done again; and there is nothing new under the sun. Take anything of which it may be said, "Look now, this is new." Already, long before our time, it existed. Only no memory remains of earlier times, just as in times to come next year itself will not be remembered.[3]

Without memory, without the bringing to mind of time, all time, and of eternity, there can be no full wisdom. The wisdom we seek first, and I think appropriately so, is an understanding of *who* we are, an understanding of the self. And yet this is already a shared question, a question inquiring into a shared identity. Not only do I or you, not only does my thinking and your thinking, have a fixed, discernible shape but so also do *we*, and *our* thinking, have a fixed, discernible shape. And so I wish to qualify the Augustinian question with which we shall begin. I wish to pluralize it, and ask: "And we, who are we?"

For any one of a number of admittedly serious reasons, the attempt to discern and to trace the common self of our times presents itself as a questionable, perhaps untenable, project. Is there indeed such a thing as a "common self" or a "times" which actually form a shared, coherent, intelligible context for individual thought and action? Questionable enough, it would seem, is the pursuit of self-knowledge without the interminably complicating addition of human plurality, the expansion from the "I" to the "we." However, it is not a matter of artificially compiling the public self from actually and appropriately unitary selves; rather, it is a matter of noticing that "we" already are, that the public realm and the public self are as real as, in fact more real than, the private. We may recall Heidegger's escape from the Husserlian entrapment of consciousness within self-consciousness in his assertion that it is not a genuine concern whether and how our consciousness might become world-consciousness, namely, whether and how we might reach our world, simply because we are already there. Correspondingly, the passage from private self-consciousness to public self-consciousness is theoretically inevitable. The burden of proof falls upon those who would claim to be equal to holding the two apart or to denying the one or the other. There is at least a theoretical necessity to the encounter between the private self and the public self, for they are inseparable. Thus to inquire into the one is to inquire into the other.

Until now I have spoken of times and selves, neither of which are as precise and as fruitful for our discussion as the Aristotelian understanding of "character." What I intend to say is that "we moderns" have a character, whatever our characters as individuals may be, and that this shared character may be inquired into and understood and spoken of. In fact, self-knowledge requires inquiry and insight into it. To know that it exists is, in practice, to recognize it, to experience recognition through its being held up. To pass from uniqueness to uniqueness without noticing the common, the shared, and the dependent is to imagine a world of isolation and freedom that doesn't exist and to deny the all-too-evident world which closes in around us.

Before we speak of public or shared character, we would do well to reflect briefly on the meaning of individual character in Aristotle. Two claims are central to Aristotle's analysis of character and are equally crucial here: character is a matter of habit and character is finally fashioned by one's theoretical understanding of human possibility and impossibility. First, character is a matter of habit. Conduct shapes character (or the peculiar person one becomes); and the peculiar person one becomes shapes conduct. This circularity of conduct and character is simply the quite familiar circularity of habit. As soon as one begins to act, patterns are established and precedents set which begin to describe and determine never what is literally possible and impossible but rather what comes easily and what comes only with difficulty, namely, what is personally pleasant and what is personally painful. After a while a life acquires a relatively fixed and stable state, a second nature, which is only to say that freedom is ordinarily lost in its exercise and that one becomes defined by one's choices and thus becomes a rather definite sort of person. To know what one, as a rule, does and says and thinks and prefers is to know specifically what sort of person one is; and the reverse is equally true. Eventually conduct accounts for character and character accounts for conduct.

To speak of second nature or character, however, is not to speak of nature. For Aristotle, a thing's nature generally describes its possibilities and its necessities, which come to the same thing. For example, by nature an acorn cannot become an elephant or a rose and, unless some impediment violently interferes with its coming-to-be, it will by nature and of necessity become an oak tree. So also for other inanimate as well as animate beings—with the exception of man. A stone, says Aristotle, released from one's hand falls; and a flame, in the free air, rises, naturally, necessarily; and

> the stone which by nature moves downwards cannot be habituated to move upwards, not even if one tries to train it by throwing it up ten thousand times; nor can fire be habituated to move downwards, nor can anything else that by nature behaves in one way be trained to behave in another.[4]

Not so with man who, when his life is genuinely his to dispose of and is not caught entirely in the grip of necessity, is an ethical being, a creature of habit (*ēthos* being the Greek word for habit). With respect to the movement and direction of a man's coming-to-be, a more appropriate metaphor than that of a stone's falling or that of a flame's rising is that of a man's hurling a stone[5] or of a man's launching an arrow.[6] From the first, the force and aim are at the individual's discretion; but we should notice how, once the stone and arrow are airborne, that force and aim have become final. Beforehand there is no necessity to their sailing in this direction or that, up or down; but their path, once given, becomes their necessity. So also in the case of the individual man's life, there is no necessity to one's doing this or that or to one's becoming this or that sort of person; the possibilities range, in classical terms, from the bestial to the godly, from the demonic to the divine. But as soon as one acts, which is as soon as one breathes, one's life becomes its own necessity, its own second nature.

The second claim of Aristotle regarding human character, which we mentioned briefly above, is that character is finally fashioned by one's theoretical understanding of human possibility and impossibility. Every action implies choice, choice for and choice against. Human individuation, the process of becoming someone in particular, involves the continuous exclusion of alternatives. And choice is always at least intentionally for the better. Furthermore, Aristotle is right, it seems, in claiming that "better" implies "best" or that choice is intelligible only against the horizon of some conception, articulate or inarticulate, explicit or implicit, of the most that can be desired and sought after. What this means is that every individual life, each instance of human coming-to-be, unfolds deliberately towards its highest conceivable completion or perfection. A man is defined by his longings and his longings, in turn, are defined by his conception of what might be longed for. When Aristotle distinguishes between the life of enjoyment, the life of virtue, and the life of wisdom—three paradigmatic states of character—he is finally distinguishing between three distinct understandings of human fullness, three distinct horizons of the humanly possible. Each man lives as far as he can see and with a view towards happiness or well-being. For Aristotle it goes without saying that every man chooses what is more pleasant and is thus sincere, truthful to his own innate preferences. What is genuinely decisive is what one is able to conceive of and thus experience as pleasant. For example, the sensualist chooses the physical embodiments of beauty to the virtual exclusion of all else because he is not alive to and thus cannot conceive of the pain of dishonor and the pleasure of acting rightly, the limit case for Aristotle being that of battlefield courage, where for the honorable man to suffer death for the defense of one's city is quite literally less painful than a cowardly escape to safety.

To speak of character, then, is not to speak of nature, which according to Aristotle is a quite optional matter for man; rather, it is to speak of second nature, of the inevitability of habit, the inevitability of a life's taking on, after a while, a rather fixed, discernible shape. A stone once it leaves one's hand or an arrow once it leaves the bow embodies a certain aim and its trajectory is immediately predictable. Its course describes an arc, a rounded-off, finite space limited by its beginnings. To act is to choose and to choose is to direct one's life towards the only conception of fullness one knows; and, in so directing one's life, that fullness and those actions appropriate to it become characteristic of one's self.

Suppose that we read Aristotle's analysis of the origin and development of individual character or individuation as an account of the origin of the cave presented in parable fashion in the *Republic* of Plato. The light of the cave is artificial, man-made, as are also the objects held up before it. Similarly, character is man-made; and it is the process of one's coming-to-be which ordinarily constitutes the light in which all else is seen. But the parable of the cave is a parable of the *polis*, of life in common, and not of individual life. And what this suggests is that character is shared and thus that no one begins his life afresh, no one forms his character alone. If the shaping of character begins as soon as one begins to act, then one's earliest conceptions of human excellence and fullness and well-being are all but decisive in placing the horizon towards which one's life thenceforth unfolds; and one's earliest understandings of what is possible and impossible, of the reaches of human expectation, are hardly critical and hardly one's own. Rather, the lives, the characters and their implicit understandings of the humanly possible, in the presence of which one's soul first opens, one's mind first thinks, and one's heart first loves, prejudice one's beginnings and provide one with an already fixed range and ranking of alternatives, an already all-but-formed character. Thus, Socrates preferred to speak with the youth of Athens; and both Plato and Aristotle attach supreme political importance to *paideia*,[7] the introduction of the young to the full range of being and to the full light of reason.

Every life, each human character, represents an opinion regarding the humanly possible and appropriate, the pleasant and the beautiful and the good, a partial truth towards which the individual is understandably partial, a good of which the individual is fond. Insofar as everyone is presumably involved in becoming someone in particular and so in fashioning a character, everyone is presumably a lover of opinion, a *philodoxos*. But cities and peoples also have opinions of their own of which they are fond, opinions which describe the objects of those shared desires and fears which have brought and keep them together. And the opinions of the city or a people are of far more decisive significance than are those of individuals. Plato likens these shared public opinions and the shared character which they fashion to a "great beast" whose likes and dislikes account fully for the opinions of its keepers, its own best spokesmen, who, in Jung's phrase, live on the leading edge of contemporary experience.[8] And Plato describes the roar of this beast as follows:

> Why, when, I said, the multitude are seated together in assemblies or in courtrooms or in theaters or camps or any other public gathering of a crowd, and with loud uproar censure some of the things that are said and done and approve of others, both in excess, with full-throated clamor and clapping of hands, and thereto the rocks and the region round about re-echoing redouble the din of the censure and the praise. In such case how do you think the young man's heart, as the saying is, is moved within him? What private teaching do you think will hold out and not rather be swept away by the torrent of censure and applause, and borne off on its current, so that he will affirm the same thing that they do to be honorable and base, and will do as they do, and be even such as they?[9]

Who or what represents, we might ask, the great Sophist, the great beast of our society and who articulates its likes and dislikes to us? What could be called "public teaching" today? We may recall that, for Aristotle, character and ethics are the appropriate concerns only of those whose lives are somehow at their own disposal, those whose lives unfold in accord with their own choices and preferences, namely, those who do and say what they do and say because they wish to, not because they have to. Most men live under the constant press of necessity and it is the sum of their necessities that account for what we see them do and hear them say. When Plato speaks of the great beast as the assembly, we must recall that only free men, men freed from private necessity and thus free for public concerns, sat in the assembly. Correspondingly, we might regard "thinkers" as the most accessible and most representative public assembly of our society where the political has become politics, a matter of calculating immediate self-interest, barely free of necessity. Presumably modern literature, particularly philosophical writing, forms a genuinely public assembly where what is said is not the child of base need. The claim here is that modern thought regarding the humanly possible, namely, modern "political thought" in the classical sense of political, has a peculiar character, with characteristic likes and dislikes and represents a coherent, intelligible opinion regarding human fullness and well-being. It is clearly impossible to trace every line in the modern countenance but a few bold, heavy lines and a few details, admittedly at the risk or cost of caricature, might provide a recognizable portrait and such recognition of our shared character is at least a step towards self-knowledge to which the Delphic injunction, I presume, still holds.

We will begin our sketch of the modern character with Descartes whose works, as conduct, were among the first to fashion that character. It is significant that his *Discourse on Method* is, by his own account, a product of isolation. Far from the peripatetic conversations of Socrates in the free, open air, the context for Descartes' discourse is a military campaign in the dead of winter and, more specifically, a warm room far from the conversations of others. He sets out upon his reflections, he says, "like a man who walks alone in the darkness."[10] Although he is not a child and has received the finest education available, Descartes sees himself as beginning altogether afresh in his reflections upon the beautiful, the good, and the true. The sum of his prior studies was not the Socratic knowledge of his own ignorance but rather the radical knowledge that there is simply no such thing as wisdom in the classical sense, namely, there is no such thing as the simply beautiful, the simply good, or the simply true. His "course of studies" in the "world of books," which he likens to the experience of foreign travel, proved finally an intolerable scandal to Descartes, who "was always eager to learn to distinguish truth from falsehood so that [he] could make intelligent decisions about the affairs of this life and act with greater confidence."[11] For so far from there being consensus or commonly shared opinions among the learned, Descartes says that he "had discovered in college that one cannot imagine anything so strange and unbelievable but that it has been held by some philosopher; and in [his] travels [he] had found that those who held opinions contrary to ours were neither barbarians nor savages, but that many of them were at least as reasonable as ourselves."[12] So, the sole, concluding insight to be drawn from books, the book of the world, the book of custom, the book of common opinion, is that there is nothing to be learned from others or "the other." Education is a gamut of despair which leaves one finally alone with the sole responsibility and possibility of studying oneself.

When Descartes says that he has always been eager to distinguish the true from the false with a view towards making intelligent, confident decisions, we may assume that his understanding of ethical wisdom was quite classical. This means that before one acts, in prospect of acting, some actions are just and others are unjust. The individual is as free to act wrongly as rightly but he is not at all free to fix the terms of wrong or right. With reference to our earlier discussion, one is free to determine one's character, indeed such freedom is inescapable; but independently of intention and preference, some characters are noble and others are base, some are in accord with human nature and others defy human nature. "Intelligent decisions about the affairs of this life" are, then, informed decisions, decisions informed by insight into the true and the false. It is precisely this possibility of moral insight of which Descartes has despaired; a person is not noble or base according to whether he does noble or base deeds, rather, deeds are noble or base according to who does them. Furthermore, all things being a matter of fashion or custom or example or preference, "the thing which pleased us ten years ago and perhaps will please us again ten years in the future, now seems extravagant and ridiculous."[13] Moral insight and all insight, for that matter, is an illusion; for there is no intellectual sight, no common intelligible world to which reason provides access, no shared light of day illuminating a shared world.

Because the character of one's deeds and not the quality of one's intentions classically determined one's character, namely, because to do base deeds was to be a base man, Aristotle claims that one should never act in doubt regarding the rightness of what one is about to do. However, since for Descartes doubt is the natural conclusion of reflection and insight, and moral wisdom an illusion, as his "second maxim" he resolves:

> . . . to be as firm and determined in my actions as I could be, and not to act on the most doubtful decisions, once I had made them, any less resolutely than on the most certain. In this matter I patterned my behavior on that of travelers, who, finding themselves lost in a forest, must not wander about, now turning this way, now that, and still less should remain in one place, but should go as straight as they can in the direction they first select and not change the direction except for the strongest reason. By this method, even if the direction was chosen at random, they will presumably arrive at some destination, not perhaps where they would like to be, but at least where they will be better off than in the middle of the forest. Similarly, situations in life often permit no delay; and when we cannot determine the course which is certainly best, we must follow the one which is probably the best; and when we cannot determine even that, we must nevertheless select one and follow it thereafter as though it were certainly the best. If the course selected is not indeed a good one, at least the reasons for selecting it are excellent. This frame of mind freed me also from the repentance and remorse commonly felt by those vacillating individuals who are always seeking as worthwhile things which they later judge to be bad.[14]

In reflecting upon this altogether central advice from Descartes, we must recall that he has already assured us that we are in the normal order of things when we cannot determine even the probably best course and thus when our initial step from the forest of radical doubt is altogether random. However, what he describes is the peculiar freedom and confidence that follows from random, that is, radically nonrational, unintelligible, and thus radically private, behavior. Altogether characteristic of modern thought is the relief and assurance of deciding that classical thought aimed too high and that a more appropriate lowering of one's sights places wisdom within our immediate and immanent possession. The qualified assertions of classical philosophy, always pervaded with measured doubt, seem now to represent mere intellectual scrupulosity which contains a right sense of pervasive inadequacy but a groundless sense of guilt or responsibility for this inadequacy.

Descartes reforms traditional thought as Luther reformed traditional belief by speaking of radical doubt and radical confidence just as Luther spoke of radical guilt and radical acceptance. Both, by a fever-therapy of sorts, follow their unsettlements to their limit and find in their fullest expression new grounds for assurance and for speaking once again of wisdom and justification respectively. From an Aristotelian perspective it is adolescent to love as if one will always love and to hate as if one will always hate, for such is both loving and hating too much. And, it is the older and the wiser man, who has experienced and learned to live with contradiction and doubt, who neither loves warmly nor hates bitterly, loving as if he will one day hate and hating as if he will one day love,[15] which is to say that doubt and the knowledge of ignorance at least mean that one will "be gentler and more agreeable to [one's] companions, having the good sense not to fancy [he] knows what [he] does not know."[16] Descartes clearly proposes a reversal—wisdom belongs to the young who act boldly and intransigently while in the thickest doubt. What is equally clear is that the meaning of wisdom has changed.

The classical wisdom that begins with wonder is not the modern wisdom that begins with doubt. We must stress that when Descartes speaks of doubt he has in mind a doubt that does not admit of intellectual resolution just as when he speaks of being lost in a forest he has in mind being *really* lost, altogether without bearings. This means that there is no right path or wrong path or that there is no proper speaking of *the* path. One must lower one's sights, one's expectations, and speak of, namely, give oneself, *a* path. And only by taking a first, resolute step does one give oneself a path which henceforth is *the* path, the only path invested with the truth of commitment and resolution.

The first point of advice, then, which Descartes would offer to one so lost is to despair of the very possibility of ever finding one's bearings and to take one step, one step free of illusion, arbitrary in the most literal sense of being grounded only in the sheer willfulness of the act. One such step will give to one's life a path, a direction described by two points, one's two feet. The one foot is the self that exists and the other is the self that knows its own existence, i.e., knows itself as existing; and the two are one being, one self. In the act of self-consciousness the self opens up an inner space, an inner world with a light and a truth all its own. How novel this response is, or at least how uncharacteristic it is of Descartes' own intellectual and spiritual fathers, might be suggested by calling to mind Dante's response to this same image and experience of being lost in a forest. You will recall that Dante begins his *Divine Comedy* alone, lost in a forest:

> Midway in our life's journey, I went astray
> from the straight road and woke to find myself
> alone in a dark wood.[17]

And the path that he follows, his ascent from hell, through purgatory, to heaven brings him to a point where, he says, my powers rest and where

> already I could feel my being turned—
> instinct and intellect balanced equally
>
> as a wheel whose motion nothing jars—
> by the Love that moves the Sun and the other stars.[18]

Whatever else one might say, it is clear that the path taken by Descartes and the path taken by Dante are not the same path. The one leads to "the love that moves the Sun and the other stars" and the other leads to the light of self-consciousness which moves the self and seeks to re-create the face of the earth. Of this latter light, viewed not in prospect with Bacon as a vision of instauration but rather viewed in retrospect with our fellows as a vision of unaccountable power, we may say that it encountered a darkness which it could not withstand, and which one might even claim it alone released fully. The "thinking thing," divorced from the "mindless thing," has been overwhelmed and denied. Instinct and intellect, matter and mind, which for Dante "balanced equally" after his path of "high fantasy," are for Descartes forever severed the one from the other after his path of "radical doubt." In Descartes, high fantasy and universal science are set off against each other and there begins a cosmic feud which puts man at odds with himself and his world, a feud in which he learns again the meaning of the curse of Cain.

In Descartes we doubtless encounter a critical turning point in the history of thinking. In his writings the bow is strung and the arrow of modern thought is launched, its arc described. And yet we can hardly hope or pretend to trace here and now the full reach of that arc, to notice what it embraces and what it excludes, what it renders likely and what unlikely, what conceivable and what all but inconceivable. We must instead drive to the center of that turning point, catch the archer's squint as the arrow leaves the bow; and it is Descartes himself who will lead us to that center and reveal to us what is surely one of the great and simple images in the presence of which the heart of modern man first opened and formed its loves. The image itself was given to Descartes in a dream which he carefully recorded and interpreted in a text entitled the *Olympica.* The *Olympica* is no longer extant and yet we have a full account of its contents preserved for us by M. Baillet in his *Vie de monsieur des Cartes* (1691). And it is upon this account that we will now reflect briefly.

In the winter of 1619 Descartes was twenty-three, a philosopher brimming with intellectual and scientific enthusiasm and a soldier in the army of Maximilian, weary after the battle of Prague. On the night of November 10, 1619, the Eve of St. Martin's, a night of usual drunkenness and revelry (though Descartes assures us that he had had no wine at all for three months), Descartes was in winter retirement in quarters near Ulm. It was on that night that Descartes experienced what he saw as a revelation from God, a revelation to him of his vocation and of the foundations of the Admirable Science which it was his calling to found and to develop. This revelation, a chain of three dreams, marked, in his own mind, the turning point in his thought and, we might add, marks, in our minds, the turning point in modern thought.

Before falling asleep, Descartes resolved to examine all of his beliefs and to let this critical examination ground his future thought and science. The first two dreams, he thinks, speak to him of his past life. The first dream describes Descartes lopsided in his stride with a great weakness in his right side. When he struggles to straighten himself he is caught by a whirlwind and spun around; but what terrifies him most is the constant fear and sensation of falling as he drags himself along leaning so far to the left.[19] This image tells of a deep divorce within him. Only one side of him is able to move and the other side brings weakness and fear and shame. His stride is not whole but lopsided and lame. In his second dream he is awakened by what he thinks is a clap of thunder and as he opens his eyes he perceives the room showered with brilliant, fiery sparks. Here too we glimpse perhaps an image of dissipated power which is unable to sustain itself. In these two dreams Descartes saw images of his past, of his being lost in a dark wood; and it is in his final dream that he finds the vision and power that is to be his, and ours.

Descartes says of the third dream, unlike the first two dreams, that it contained nothing terrifying. In the third dream he comes across a book on his table and when he sees that it is a dictionary he is delighted, hoping that it will indeed be useful. Just then he comes across another book and finds it to be a collection of poems entitled *Corpus Poetarum* (The Collected Works of the Poets). Curious, Descartes opens the book to the line *"Quod vitae sectabor iter?"* (What path in life shall I take?).[20] At the same moment a man whom he does not know offers him some verses beginning with the words *Est et Non* (Is and is not, yes and no, being and nonbeing). Quite simply, these are two books and not one. It is the dictionary which stands for all the sciences in one, the universal science, and in which Descartes delights. Raising and responding to the question "What path in life shall I take?" is the work of the poets whose characteristic and proper response to any path, to any individual life tangled in the ambiguity and incompleteness of becoming, to any word spoken, to any deed done, is always "*est et non*," yes and no, it is and it is not.

To quit the world of the poets, the realm of what always both is and is not, is to quit the realm of ambiguity, imperfection, and becoming. Science is certainty, hard and fast and changeless. The truth descends upon Descartes with the sudden, unprovoked brilliance of a lightning flash; and his calling is to gather into one again the fiery and luminous power of that revelation. Science is to be the work of one man and Descartes' own calling is to be that man. The past, tradition, whatever already is and has been preserved, must become for him as a void, as chaos, so that he might alone create afresh the certain order of being and knowing. What light there was outside of and beyond this work has spent itself in an impotent shower and vanished. The new light must unfold from within the blazing solitude of this one man's and this one night's moment. New wine is poured for a new feast. I invoke theological imagery for a vision conceived and developed by Descartes in implicitly theological categories. The movement of modern thought is in so many respects the founding of a new religion, minus a god whom one can invoke or at least one who can be trusted to check one's madness, perhaps minus a god at all.

After Descartes, if one follows this thinking and its implicit counsel, it can be nothing but an illusion to speak of *paideia*, or *vocatio*, or the *imitatio Christi*. Each life properly begins itself afresh, encounters itself radically alone and thus at its own origins as well as at the origins of its world. This endeavor to begin all things afresh is, regrettably for Descartes, at once compromised by the fact that we are children, dependent on others for our beginnings, before we are adults capable of radical doubt, the exclusion of all dependence, and the lucid, willful founding of ourselves and our world. This he regards as a manifest imperfection with which one must make shift just as an architect must accept the fact that he cannot raze an entire city and rebuild it around and in accord with the sense of form and beauty embodied in the new structures he intends to raise up. The ideal remains, however, to deny the prior and independent character of the whole and to see that it unfolds exclusively from one's own self-assertion. There will, there can, be Truth and Beauty and Goodness at the same time only if they proceed from the consciousness of a single self.

We may well question whether Descartes has, after all, lowered human sights by proposing as human ideality what classical philosophy and theology saw as divine reality—self-thinking thought. And yet, for man, the content of this thought seems only to be the doubting of all else but the self which, in turn, is merely the negation of all else but the self, and so on. In what might be seen as a mimicking of the divine reality, as thought of by the ancients, the Cartesian self calls itself into existence by doubting, by denying all else; and the classical ideal to know all things comes to mean nothing because all things mean nothing. Wisdom is as inaccessible to man as it was thought to be for God. While it is true that he speaks of *a* path, one must live as if it is *the* path, which is to say that one must create the fullness of being, the Truth, the Beauty, the Goodness, the One of which one seemed to glimpse nothing and of which one consequently despaired. Descartes has transformed wisdom into a work, a project, a making, a determinate problem, for he denies that he can work with anything else.

In speaking of the traditionally highest objects of human aspiration as originating in the kinetic activity of the self and thus as somehow the object of human design and making, Descartes has denied the most fundamental distinctions of classical thought, the distinction between the man-made and the non-man-made and so the distinction between mortal and immortal, human and divine, or, in Christian, Jewish, or Islamic terms, between creature and creator. What this means is that the whole becomes the proper object of *poiēsis* or art or human making, the only inner sight or *eidos* is that of the craftsman which he works out in the raw material of the nonself. Primitive and classical men surely know of *poiēsis*, the experience of human making. What is characteristically modern and innovative is not *poiēsis* and *technē* (the knowing or seeing that accompanies *poiēsis*), but rather the extension of the appropriate scope of *poiēsis* and *technē* to encompass the whole of the nonself, the whole of reality beyond the definition of particular human character, namely, human nature and the natural world. The movement from the image of one lost in a forest to the image of the architect leads us from self-assertion as radical doubt to self-assertion as power. And it becomes crucial to reflect with care upon human making and the *eidos* of the craftsman, which we will attempt to do when we return to modern thinking in a later chapter.

For now, we are attempting no more than to make a first lucid and critical acquaintance with ourselves as peculiarly modern and Western. We are telling some of the stories of our shared past so that we might slowly come to recognize ourselves in a theater greater and older than the assembly where the roar of the great beast prevails. It is my conviction that Descartes articulates and embraces and perhaps in some sense originates the vision which has shaped our common character and greatly limited the number and the meaning of those possibilities which present themselves to us when we ask ourselves, "What path in life shall we take?" And yet the recognition we seek may be more accessible and telling when we encounter a less formidable, less complex, and less oblique embodiment of our common character than Descartes. I have three in mind, three quite popular "heroes" from contemporary literature; and we will reflect upon each in turn in the hope of coming to a still sharper and fuller insight into ourselves. They are: Thomas More in Robert Bolt's *A Man for All Seasons*, Don Quixote in Dale Wasserman's *Man of La Mancha*, and finally Jean-Baptiste Clamence in Albert Camus' *The Fall*.

Robert Bolt, in his introduction to *A Man for All Seasons*, admits that Thomas More was a Christian saint and admits, likewise, that he, Bolt, has little or no appreciation of what it could mean to be either a Christian or a saint. So, he says, he has seen fit to turn the historical Thomas More into a modern hero, "a hero of selfhood."[21]

> At any rate [he says], Thomas More, as I wrote about him, became for me a man with an adamantine sense of his own self. He knew where he began and left off, what area of himself he would yield to the encroachments of his enemies, and what to the encroachments of those he loved. It was a substantial area in both cases, for he had a proper sense of fear and was a busy lover. Since he was a clever man and a great lawyer he was able to retire from those areas in wonderfully good order, but at length he was asked to retreat from that final area where he located his self. And there this supple, humorous, unassuming, and sophisticated person set like metal, was overtaken by an absolutely primitive rigor, and could no more be budged than a cliff.[22]

What ensues is the story of a martyr not to the truth of Christianity but to the truth of his own self. Perjury, not apostasy, is the unforgiveable sin against the Holy Spirit which More refuses to commit and for which refusal he is executed. We may recall that his only objection to Roper, his daughter Margaret's suitor, is not that he is a Lutheran and is thus a heretic but rather that Roper is unsure of himself and vacillates regularly. "Listen, Roper," says More, "two years ago you were a passionate Churchman; now you're a passionate—Lutheran. We must pray that when your head's finished turning, your face is front again."[23] More himself is uncertain regarding the truth of Christianity and the falsity of Lutheranism which is what he admits when his lifelong friend Norfolk argues that it makes no sense for More to be throwing his life away for an opinion or a theory. More responds as follows:

> The Apostolic Succession of the Pope is—
> . . . Why, it's a theory, yes; you can't see
> it, you can't touch it; it's a theory.
> But what matters to me is not whether it's
> true or not but that I believe it to be true,
> or rather, not that I *believe* it, but that
> *I* believe it.[24]

Similarly, as a lawyer, he makes no claims to be able to distinguish between the just and the unjust. "The currents and eddies of right and wrong . . . I can't navigate. I'm no voyager. But in the thickets of the law, oh, there I'm a forester. I doubt if there's a man alive who could follow me there, thank God."[25]

It is significant that Bolt's More gives no account of himself to his family or to his friends. He never suggests that what binds him does or ought to bind them; for his truths are admittedly theories until transfigured by the force of commitment which is simply arbitrary, private, and unshareable. He cannot teach or inspire or recommend his way, for his way is his own self available to no one else. The best he can do to be a friend, when friendship is inevitably without common ground and is thus but illusion and "sloth," is what he does for Norfolk when he picks a quarrel and asks

> And what would you do with a water spaniel that was afraid of water? You'd hang it! Well, as a spaniel is to water, so is a man to his own self. I will not give in because I oppose it—I do—not my pride, not my spleen, nor any other of my appetites but *I* do *I*——Is there no single sinew in the midst of this that serves no appetite of Norfolk's but is just Norfolk? There is! Give *that* some exercise, my lord.[26]

In *Man of La Mancha*, Cervantes blocks out the prison production of his tale of Don Quixote and sets the initial scene by announcing:

> Here is an example of how to the untrained eye one thing may seem to be another. To Sancho an inn. To Quixote a castle. To someone else whatever his mind may make of it. But for the sake of argument, let us grant Sancho *his* vision. An inn. . . .[27]

And so begins a story of vision and dream in which Don Quixote, mad and yet thereby the child of God, endeavors to do what all men must do—"add some measure of grace to the world."[28] To surrender dreams and vision is a greater madness; for life without the grace of mad vision is without beauty or warmth or grace; and men, when faced by death ask why, not why must they die but why must they have lived.[29]

In the present scheme of things it is death not life that makes sense, death not life that goes without saying. Quixote tampers with the scheme of things and inns become castles, shaving basins become golden helmets, windmills become giants, an old man becomes a knight, and a whore becomes a lady. Around this last transformation of Aldonza to Dulcinea revolves the entire drama. Aldonza at first desperately resists his calling her a lady as a deeper violation than any she has suffered from her customers. She pleads with him to see her as she clearly is, as she knows herself to be and as others know her. She begs him to take another look. Don Quixote refuses, explaining only that he has already seen her in his heart.[30] He forces his grace upon her and she succumbs. Don Quixote is a craftsman for whom prior form is to be denied and annihilated so that he might work freely with unformed material. "Facts," he says, "are the enemy of truth."[31] And he is the enemy of facts, of the given, of all that claims to be beautiful or ugly independently of him as a particular beholder. It is important to note in passing that Don Quixote may be attractive only because his vision seems to be a clear improvement over the naked eye, only because his truth improves the facts in this case. But, in principle, it could have just as easily been a matter of transforming a lady into a whore. In fact, in most cases, it is. Both More and Quixote seem to appeal to what is noblest and most excellent, but their own stands are finally ambiguous and only privately secure.

The most fully lucid and decidedly ethical rendering of the modern character is, in my judgment, to be found in Camus' last completed novel, *The Fall*. *The Fall* is, at once, the confession and the self-assertion of one man, Jean-Baptiste Clamence, the voice of one crying in a new secular wilderness of his own making. Clamence, in a denial as radical and sweeping and final as Descartes' doubt, refuses the claims, the gestures, the questions, the appeals of those who exist quite freely and independently of him. He allows the world to reenter his consciousness, as he allows his mistresses to enter his bedroom, but only in response to his call, his needs, and his desires. He insists not that his mistresses love him, for this would establish a mutual claim to recognition and acceptance, but only that his mistresses remain faithful to him, not that he pretends to remain faithful in return. In this way his own existence is affirmed and confirmed without any corresponding affirmation of a world, an otherness, human and inhuman, quite beyond him. His happiness and well-being hangs upon this imbalance, this desired distance from any communion with otherness. Jean-Baptiste himself quite tellingly sums up the governing desire or intent of his life, which he often realizes is a desire for lofty places, a desire to be God:

> On my own admission, I could live happily only on condition that all the individuals on earth, or the greatest possible number, were turned toward me, eternally in suspense, devoid of independent life and ready to answer my call at any moment, doomed in short to sterility until the day I should deign to favor them. In short, for me to live happily it was essential for the creatures I chose not to live at all. They must receive their life, sporadically, only at my bidding.[32]

The world of Clamence is a recognizably Cartesian world if we understand, as we must, Cartesian wisdom as a possibility for human becoming, a possibility for being, for living as well as for thinking. We may notice it is cold and damp and solitary and manmade. The earth (streets), the sea (canals), and the sky mingle confusedly and the only lines to be drawn sharply are those in consciousness; and they are drawn defiantly and intransigently. Clamence rules, or seeks to rule, this place of confusion and reversal. We may recall another such man with similar ambitions, King Creon in *Antigone*. Creon refuses burial to the dead and sentences the living to be buried alive. He thinks his rule extends so far that he may reverse the orders and the kingdoms of the living and the dead. He arrogantly puts off the entreaties and warnings of his wife, his son, his son's bride-to-be, and his subjects, asking with rhetorical scorn if a man should listen to his wife, a father to his son, a man to a woman, a king to his subjects. Finally, his son comments with searing ferocity, "You'd rule a desert beautifully alone,"[33] which is precisely the character of his rule soon afterwards, once his wife, his son, and his son's bride have destroyed themselves. This place of Clamence is hell. Camus is altogether clear on that as Descartes was not. Camus begins with the concentric canals of Amsterdam, the circles of hell, at the very center of which Clamence dwells and has his being. Clamence, make no mistake, is Satan, radical, pure, embodied evil. The path of modern thought becomes clear only when it has come to term and we must face ourselves. It is a fall, the fall of Adam. In hell, the character of evil is stripped of pretense and one sees it straight on. Sin is the imitation of God. What is sinful is not what one would never catch God doing, not what God would never do, but what God alone properly does. God alone bestows life and death and the meaning of each life and death. God alone decides what it means to be a tree, or a river, or a child, or a murderer. God alone judges and suspends judgment. Finally, God alone enjoys the sight of evil and suffering and laughs alone at the shattering of the universe. Only God is able to rule a desert *beautifully* alone, to bring the desert to blossom and the dry bones to rise up. When modern man knows himself not as God but as one who would be God, there occurs a moment of recognition, painful and resented, a moment Camus described in the frontispiece of this his own last work with these words of Lermontov:

> Some were dreadfully insulted, and quite seriously, to have held up as a model such an immoral character as *A Hero of Our Time*; others shrewdly noticed that the author had portrayed himself and

> his acquaintances. . . . *A Hero of Our Time*, gentlemen, is in fact a portrait, but not of an individual; it is the aggregate of the vices of our whole generation in their fullest expression.

In man's hell there is no metaphor, no ambiguity, nothing that does not either exist or not exist. "Yes," explains Clamence, "hell must be like that: streets filled with shop signs and no way of explaining oneself. One is classified once and for all."[34] There is no becoming and no shared recognition of becoming, no fellowship, no communion. For the wise, i.e., the powerful, there is pity without absolution, understanding without forgiveness, while for the weak there is "the melancholy of the common condition and the despair of not being able to escape it."[35] For the few whose sin is fully lucid there is the possibility of adoration.

This haunt of Clamence, and of ours, is all but uninhabitable. It is a world fashioned and sustained by denials, betrayals, and lies. As such it is as precarious as is any deception so long as the truth remains accessible and there are still those not yet fully deceived. With each new generation this hell must be populated and repopulated by conversion, a peculiarly thorough conversion formalized into education, which is the focus of our next reflections. For now we might only recall that *The Fall* describes such an attempt at conversion, an attempt which fails. The listener simply walks away at the end. Clamence, worked up but not weeping, concedes that he has only a solution and not an ideal. "But," he adds excitedly,

> when you don't like your own life, when you know that you must change lives, you don't have any choice, do you? What can one do to become another? Impossible. One would have to cease being anyone, forget oneself for someone else, at least once. But how?[36]

Clamence has left us with a most urgent question. He inquires into the possibility of resistance, the possibility of resisting the mere abstraction we have made of ourselves and of the world, an abstract affirmation rooted in and never escaping the fundamental doubt and denial which spawned it, and the possibility of encountering, embracing, and becoming something other and something new. This we call resistance and perhaps all that we or Clamence may find within our common character to say to one another of such a possibility is:

> Come now, admit that you would be flabbergasted if a chariot came down from heaven to carry me off, or if the snow suddenly caught fire. You don't believe it? Nor do I. But still I must go out.[37]

And so must we go out, on the soul's trek abroad.

NOTES

1. Augustine *Confessions* 10.6, trans. F. W. Sheed (New York: Sheed & Ward, 1942), p. 177.
2. William Shakespeare, *Macbeth,* act 5, sc. 6, ll. 26–28.
3. Ecclesiastes, 1:9–11. This and all further biblical texts, unless otherwise indicated, are from *The Jerusalem Bible* (New York: Doubleday, 1967).
4. Aristotle *Nichomachean Ethics* 2. 1. 1103a21–23, trans. W. D. Ross, in *Collected Works*, ed. Richard McKeon (New York: Random House, 1941).
5. See ibid., 3. 5. 1114a–1719.
6. See ibid., 1. 2. 1094a–2425.
7. For a brilliant account of the Greek understanding of *paideia* see Werner Jaeger, *Paideia: The Ideals of Greek Culture*, trans. Gilbert Highet (New York: Oxford University Press, 1939–45).
8. C. G. Jung, *Modern Man in Search of a Soul* (London, 1969), pp. 196ff.
9. Plato *Republic* 492b–d, trans. Paul Shorey, in *Plato: The Collected Dialogues*, ed. Edith Hamilton and Huntington Cairns, Bollingen Series no. 71 (New York: Pantheon Books, 1961).
10. René Descartes, *Discourse on Method* 2. 17, in René Descartes, *Philosophical Essays*, trans. Laurence J. Lafleur (Indianapolis: Bobbs-Merrill, 1964). Copyright © 1964 by The Bobbs-Merrill Company, Inc. Reprinted by permission of the publisher.
11. Ibid., 1. 10.
12. Ibid., 2. 16.
13. Ibid.
14. Ibid., 2. 24–25.
15. See Aristotle *Rhetoric* 2. 12–13. 1389a–1390a.
16. Plato *Theaetetus* 210c, trans. F. M. Cornford, in *Collected Dialogues*.

17. Dante Alighieri, *The Inferno*, trans. John Ciardi (New York: Mentor, 1954), p. 28.

18. Dante Alighieri, *The Paradiso*, trans. John Ciardi (New York: Mentor, 1961), p. 365.

19. It is interesting to note and to speculate over the fact that it is the left side of the brain which controls the right side of the body, Descartes' weak side in the dream, and that it is the left side of the brain which controls the powers of music, imagination, metaphor, intuition, and so many mysterious powers lost and forgotten. The right side of the brain, however, which controls the powers of analysis, logic, articulate speech, calculation, and computation, also controls the left side of the body on which Descartes, in his dream, leans for support and preservation.

20. Both of the passages which Descartes discovered in the *Corpus Poetarum* (i.e., *quod vitae sectabor iter* and *est et non*) are to be found in the *Eclogues* of the Latin poet Ausonius, in *Eclogues 2* and *4* respectively.

21. Robert Bolt, *A Man for All Seasons* (New York: Vintage, 1960), p. xiii.

22. Ibid., p. 11.

23. Ibid., p. 18.

24. Ibid., p. 53.

25. Ibid., p. 37.

26. Ibid., pp. 71–72.

27. Dale Wasserman, *Man of La Mancha* (New York: Dell, 1966), p. 48.

28. Ibid., p. 50.

29. See ibid., p. 91.

30. See ibid., p. 84.

31. Ibid., p. 74.

32. Albert Camus, *The Fall* (New York: Vintage, 1956), p. 68.

33. Sophocles *Antigone* trans. Elizabeth Wyckoff (Chicago: University of Chicago Press, 1954), l. 739.

34. Camus, p. 47.

35. Ibid., p. 143.

36. Ibid., p. 144–45.

37. Ibid., pp. 145–46.

> We must not act like sleepers. The waking have one common world, but the sleeping turn aside each into a world of his own.
>
> Heraclitus

CHAPTER THREE

RESISTING

"What path in life shall I take?" The moment one path becomes more probable than another, one's possibilities have already begun to diminish, perhaps not theoretically but with a practical necessity all but impervious to theoretical objections. And surely by the time one is capable of formulating a question as remarkably free and speculative as "What path in life shall I take?" one's more or less probable responses to that question are dreadfully diminished and, in fact, the possible paths one is likely even to conceive of will be rather narrowly select. We have already claimed and explained the claim that one's earliest understandings of human excellence and well-being describe the circumference of one's world and thus decisively place the horizon towards which one's life thenceforth unfolds. The lives, the characters, the approving and disapproving eyes and words, and their implicit understandings of the humanly possible, in the presence of which one's soul first opens, one's thoughts and words first shape themselves and, most critically, one's heart first loves—all these events which belong to one's first days and years—prejudice one's beginnings and furnish one with an already determined range and ranking of alternative possibilities, an already all-but-formed character.

This is a claim which we have already considered and which rests upon an appreciation of the inescapable circularity of conduct and character, the inescapable personal gravity created and strengthened by one's actions. In very simplest terms, deceptively familiar and trite, we are creatures of habit. A truism, but nonetheless true for its being such. What we have already once spoken or done comes a second time with more ease or with less difficulty; it becomes familiar, in time, and other possibilities become strange, to be considered and approached only with difficulty. Man, whose properly human works are for him a matter of freedom and not of necessity, a matter of habit and not of nature, nevertheless creates each time a second nature, a web of habit, which describes his personal necessities. "Habit," explains Aristotle, "is a thing not unlike nature; what happens often is akin to what happens always, natural events happening always, habitual events often . . . for as soon as a thing has become habitual, it is virtually natural."[1]

Habits and character are rarely the work of solitude and isolation. They most often grow from common soil, the fruit of early conversion and conversation. Habits bind us to one another securely and assuringly and together to a world, to a span of space and time, which we agree somehow to see and to confront and to deal with in generally shared terms. Habits and character represent a caucus of individuals pacted and bound together, knowingly or unknowingly, to be young and to age and to die together in common spaces and understandings, familiar and friendly. Habits and character reveal and express man's fundamentally political capacities, aspirations, and needs. To form a habit is to master the strange and to render it increasingly familiar and to form a character is to take one's place amidst others distinct yet inseparable, wittingly loyal, indebted to one's fathers and mothers and responsible for one's sons and daughters. It is fully appropriate, therefore, that we should reflect in some depth upon doubtlessly the most significant political document in our shared political history, Plato's *Republic*, and more specifically upon the cave parable, where Plato offers an account of the political character of habit and traces the stages of resistance to the great beast of public habit or opinion.

Socrates begins his "parable" by asking Glaukon, his young and faithful companion, to form with him an image (*apeikason* from *eikōn*, whence our "icon") in his mind; and the account which then follows represents the careful delineation of that image. What is imaged here, explains Socrates, is our natural capacity both for "education" and for what might be called "miseducation," or perhaps for "coming of age" and for "failing to come of age." The critical word here is *paideia*, which we have noticed before and which does not readily convey itself to us. Springing from the word for child, *paideia* spans the event of becoming, the raising up, the rising, of the child into the full light of day, the full being of its humanity. Most simply, *paideia* means "rearing" in the grandest sense of that word. Indeed we must expand and dream past our ordinary conceptions of rearing and education to approach the meaning of *paideia.* And *apaideusia*, the privative or negative form of this word, suggests that this process admits of failure and reversal. A child may well strain towards and be led into the full light of its dawning humanity or it may well be confined and obscured in an all but subterranean space and time where its humanity will see and be seen in the lights and shadows made and cast by likewise diminished men and their opinions. Here its humanity will never reach or even reach towards what it was to be.

Socrates begins with the state of "unbecoming," the darkened state of those denied the sun's light and so denied their own proper coming to be. His first remark regarding *apaideusia* is that we must imagine this condition as something which simply befalls us, as something endured or suffered (*toioutō pathei*) but in no way undertaken. Apart from this, Socrates says nothing about when or how or why one first enters the cave of distorted and diminished being. It is both understandable and odd that we should require or appreciate such an explanation. For the cave obviously describes the givenness of the child (*pais*), existent and unrealized, the point of departure for all human nurture and realization (*paideia*). The child is, embodies, unrealization, diminishment, sheer unreality (*apaideusia*) or what Heidegger has spoken of as *Verfallen* and *Geworfenheit*, "fallenness" and "thrownness." It is not as if the child had once been in the possession and the realization of its possibilities only to have lost its hold on them, although there is a certain experiential and not wholly explicable truth to this claim which was of peculiar interest to Plato and to Augustine, among others. Nevertheless, such is not literally the case. What *is* literally the case is that childhood is a state of "not yet having been" rather than of "once having been." As such it is a condition to be suffered as one's inevitable and at least temporary lot. It may be significant and illuminating to note that the Greek word for a young child (*paidion*), like the word for slave (*andrapodon*), is neuter. Now in ancient Greek gender the most fundamental distinction was that between animate beings, beings alive or thought to be alive, and inanimate beings. Further, to be alive meant, it would seem, to act, to move rather than to be moved, to dispose over one's possibilities. Consequently, both young children and slaves were to be regarded as inanimate, as having no life of their own at their own disposal, as beings to be moved. In short, their characteristic state was one of *pathos* or suffering.

In the light of these brief reflections, Socrates' initial comment that this image represents "some sort of befalling" becomes significantly ambiguous. The cave and the life therein may thus represent either the condition of the very young child or it may represent the condition of one who has left behind the literal childhood of age without becoming free with respect to his own life, namely, the condition of the slave. In either case the first critical time of one's life is the time when one passes from being a *paidion* to being a *pais*, the years of youth when one is either being led from the private, unknowing, speechless obscurity of one's own isolated existence and home into the common, lucid, disclosed and disclosing world of shared reflection and discourse. The second critical time of one's life would be whatever moment or moments bring with them the realization of one's own servitude to ways of thinking and speaking and living which do not permit, much less drive one towards, the freedom and fullness of being which is ours to have and to be. The dwellers of Socrates' underworld, a place and a people *atopos*, nowhere in particular, are specifiedly neither young nor old, born neither slave nor free, neither male nor female; rather, they are human beings (*anthropoi*) distinguished only by and for their slavishly illusory and diminished condition. They have been here in bonds from childhood, this much we are told; but these comments are mere stage directions which do not disclose the actual extent or character of their bondage, which is manifest only when those literal bonds from childhood are cut. Only when the captive is literally free to leave, free to ascend, does his bondage reveal itself clearly and fully.

Perhaps it would be well to recall this scene in some detail before commenting further on its significance. Socrates describes a subterranean cavelike dwelling inhabited by two classes of men: the captives and their keepers or educators. The captives have been bound from their youth to their stations along a wall which they must face and which serves as a screen for a curriculum of shadows cast upon it for their enlightenment. Behind their backs is a fire set off from them by a low wall which means that the light of the fire must find its way to their wall and to their eyes by a circuitous route of reflections off the roof of the cave. Finally, this low wall raised between the fire and the captives is used by the educators as a puppet show of sorts. The captors walk behind it on a ramp, holding up various objects which cast their shadows upon the captives' wall. The objects held up are themselves mere shadows, namely, replicas, miniatures, of creatures to be found above ground, between the earth and the sun, in the light of day. And so, the captives' experience of things is several times removed from what is usually thought of to be reality. Let us take a single example and reflect upon how they come to the knowledge of a tree. The captors construct an artificial tree, perhaps the outline of a tree carved from a piece of board or stiffened cloth. This facsimile is held up above the puppet wall between the fire's glow and the captives' gaze and its shadow, vague and rippling, rises to the wall's surface before the captives' eyes. The tree which they see coming to be before their eyes both is and is not a tree. It is the image of a tree or, more precisely, the image of an image of a tree. Yet this is the only tree the captives have ever known; and thus for them who have never even glimpsed an original, a real tree in this case, what they see cannot be seen as an image. It is, quite simply, tree. And so on with all else in their world of shadows. This is the only world they know and thus it is the world of their desires and loves and struggles.

The real bondage of the cave-dwellers is, after a while, one of habit alone, strengthened as it is shared. They are chained to this wall not by iron shackles but by the sheer inner gravity of their loves and attachments, their assumptions and familiarities. The metaphor which Socrates uses to lay open the experience and meaning of habit is, quite appropriately, the metaphor of the eye's accommodation to light and to darkness. I say "appropriately" because, as shall become clear when we discuss "seeing" fully in the next chapter, the Greeks held sight to be the purest of the senses and the most fitting metaphor for man's highest human powers and activities. Man was born to see; and to speak of sight is to speak of man straight on, with essential centeredness. Thus, we should think of the underworld bondsmen as "see-ers," which is precisely as Socrates depicts them. Their bondage is rooted in the eye's capacity to accommodate itself either to light or to darkness and thus in the capacity of the mind's eye to dwell either in truth or in illusion. For when one of the captives has his chains removed he finds himself not free but still bound to his station. Socrates says he must be compelled to move, to quit his accustomed posture. For to turn is to face the light, not straight on but more directly than before, not the light of day but still the light of the cave's fire. His eyes burn and water and contract and the new world they disclose is less distinct, less accessible, and surely less satisfying than the old. As such, it must seem less real than his own world which he once knew well and trusted and enjoyed.

Although closer to reality, our newly freed captive experiences himself to be further than he has ever been from reality. More free than ever before, he has never fought so desperately against coercion and force. And matters grow ever more desperately painful and confused as he is dragged from the cave itself through a tunnel into the light of day. The sun's brilliance, light itself, is experienced as a violent sea of blinding blackness such as envelops each of Homer's fallen heroes as they sink into death. To eyes so accustomed to darkness and illusion, light appears blacker than black and truth appears to be illusion itself. Soon, of course, this all changes; and our captive's eyes grow accustomed to the light, first the night's light and then the day's light. And between the earth and the sun he forms new ways and new loves. He is again bound, now to the sights and sounds of the earth. If he is to return, he must be dragged below the earth bringing only anger to those whose world he now finds and says to be unacceptably removed and darkened and diminished.

This image of the cave and of the "education" and "miseducation" which it images for us will accompany our reflections for the rest of this work and must await fuller commentary in due time. Surely the distinction between sunlight and cavelight, between shadows and originals, must be drawn more sharply and understood more deeply, particularly in the light of Plato's image of the divided line. However, our present concerns are more focused and limited than such questions. For now we are concerned with the nature and possibility of resisting our shared character, who we have already come to be, and of reaching towards the more and the other which we neither know nor love nor explicitly desire. In the parable of the cave, we have a tale of resistance; and we may learn from it that resistance is always a struggle with ourselves and with our own second nature. Resistance involves suspending our deepest assumptions and predilections, as well as a willingness to admit ambiguity, confusion, pain, and a deep unknowing. Finally, resistance requires that we love so blindly and at such a remove from what seems to correspond to our love that we love long and far and unrequited. It appears that Socrates assumes the need for force, assumes that no one will resist his own world and himself unless compelled. Even if we were capable of resisting once we resolved to do so, Socrates seems to suggest that we are incapable of forming such a resolve and surely of sustaining it in the face of the pain and vexation and abuse which would be ours on its account. Let us assume for a moment that this is quite literally the opinion of Socrates and that his opinion is well-founded. Let us assume further the presence of a compelling external force, a body of educators, say, one generation concerned for the right education of another, the aged concerned for the proper rearing of the young, concerned that the young should not endure the failings and limits which their fathers have known. We shall see.

It is not clear that one man can lead another to the truth, although it is manifestly clear that one man can deceive another. In fact it can be and and has been argued many times that only man, unlike stones and foxes and gods, is able to deceive and to be deceived. The lie, like tombs and symbols, seems to be unique to man. Perhaps tombs and symbols are themselves among man's most essential deceptions. Regardless, through symbol and speech, we seem to be able to introduce others into our own limits, to confine their attention as we are confined; and within any such limited world there is something to be learned and experienced. To gesture towards anything at all is both to disclose and to delimit, to beckon towards one reality while distracting and thus detracting from others. Accordingly, the captors in Socrates' underworld are indeed educators in some earnest and to some purpose. They educate or rear those born in the cave into the possibilities which are theirs and reward excellence in appropriate terms. Ordinarily, any teacher educates others into his own images; the young are, as a rule, reared into and by a tradition which, once appropriated, will render them well-suited to those peculiar realities which they will surely confront.

Each people educates its children for its own ways.

Briefly, all essential education is usually by rote which is precisely the pattern of instruction described in the cave. Education is a process of accommodation to the light, the artificial light, cast upon a place and a time to illuminate and appreciate the lives spent there always only once. Such truth must be learned by heart, laid to heart. This is a simple fact which Canassatego, an Iroquois leader, once endeavored to point out to a characteristically parochial and Faustian body of white colonials, in this case the Virginia legislature. The year is 1744 and Canassatego is responding to an invitation from the Virginia legislature to the Six Nations to send six youths gratis to the Williamsburg College of William and Mary.

> We know you highly esteem the kind of Learning taught in these Colleges, and the maintenance of our young Men, while with you, would be very expensive to you. We are convinced, therefore, that you mean to do us Good by your Proposal; and we thank you heartily. But you who are so wise must know that different Nations have different Conceptions of things; and you will not therefore take it amiss, if our Ideas of this kind of Education happen not to be the same with yours. We have had some experience of it. Several of our young People were formerly brought up in the Colleges of the Northern Provinces; they were instructed in all your Sciences; but, when they came back to us, they were bad

> Runners, ignorant of every means of living in the Woods, unable to bear either Cold or Hunger, knew neither how to build a Cabin, take a deer, or kill an enemy, spoke our language imperfectly, were therefore neither fit for Hunters, Warriors, nor Counsellors; they were totally good for nothing. We are however not the less obliged for your kind Offer, tho' we decline accepting it; and to show our grateful Sense of it, if the Gentlemen of Virginia shall send us a Dozen of their Sons, we will take great care of their Education, instruct them in all we know, and make Men of them.[2]

Indeed, different nations do have different conceptions of things and when a nation educates its young it educates them in accord with those conceptions. To be educated in accord with other conceptions is to be good for nothing. And yet that "nothing" represents all that this one people fail to know or to love or even to desire. It is not simply nothing; it is, rather, nothing they can make their own and remain who and what and where they have come to be. To educate beyond one's own conceptions, beyond the limits of one's own character, were it possible, would represent an uncertain, subversive, and high ambition. To do so would be to act irresponsibly, to act without the capacity to know and so to accept in advance the foreseeable consequences of what one is doing. As such it involves a deep risk or, perhaps, a deep trust. But to what extent is it possible?

The simple claim which underlies these reflections and which requires to be formulated more explicitly now before we explore this question of the possibility of an education in resistance[3] is that any understanding of the good and the true and the beautiful attainable by men and admitting of a vision which may be formulated and communicated so as to become the foundation and center of shared lives is inevitably partial. Aristotle seems right in saying that the soul never thinks without a mental image (*phantasma*) and that this is a matter of necessity (*anagkē*) for man, even when he thinks his most theoretical thoughts (*hotan te theōrei*).[4] What this means is that human thought and speech, and thus all communication and education, cannot avoid imagery, cannot avoid the space between what simply is and what simply is not. Such images—always partial, always provisional—become deceptions once they become dogma or teaching. True teaching, teaching which reaches towards the truth, consists in refutation, namely, in denying the denial of the truth implied in any dogma or positive teaching which thinks to deny its own limits not by transcending them but by claiming that whatever those limits fail to comprehend and do justice to is good for nothing. Refutation, in this sense, may take a range of forms. For instance, there is the experience of travel which was a critical dimension of the Sophist experience. By travel I have in mind not a touristic sweep across strange lands leaving behind the litter of condescension but rather the suspension of one's own beliefs and ways and the uncritical, sympathetic encounter with other and foreign modes of thinking and of living.

Then there is Socratic refutation in which one is led to see that to continue to hold a favored position will involve the denial of still another more deeply held truth. Thus one learns that one's opinions are mostly one-sided, mostly incomplete, and that to hold them too uncritically, too wholeheartedly is to rend the soul asunder and to leave the thinking subject without the integrity and consistency of thought which alone will center its pursuit of knowledge. Perhaps the most dramatic instance of Socratic refutation is to be found, strangely enough, in the second book of Samuel[5] where David finds himself condemning the selfish greed of the rich man in Nathan's story and, in fact, claiming that such a man deserves to die, only to be told in the end by the prophet that he, King David, is himself that very man. Finally there is the mystical refutation in which all that can be thought and spoken is negated so as to form a void which is alone thought to affirm the perfection of being.

For now I wish to focus on the first of these forms of refutation or resistance, the experience of travel. For this seems to be the most common and commonly accessible mode of resistance. We will assume that most men live political lives in the sense that they are born and spend their days mostly under the shadow of opinions and assumptions which they rarely if ever pause to question. From their youth they are bound to familiar modes of living and thinking, to a character in which they participate and which shapes their own second nature. This describes the condition of most men, young and uncritical before they are old, born in caves and accustomed to the relative darkness in which they make their own way. In brief, most men only confront and know cultural reality, reality as prismed peculiarly through one or another culture. Few if any of us have or perceive any access to reality apart from its peculiar incarnations in time. Few of us are able to conceive of human possibilities apart from precedents already testified to in the lives of others. Thus we first sense the diminished and partial character of our own understandings and experiences to be comprehensive and fully adequate when we encounter, seriously and sympathetically, the understandings and experiences of others so far from ours that our minds fall blank upon them, disbelieving and uncomprehending. Resistance usually begins when we stumble quite by chance from one cave into another—we laugh at what others there take with utter seriousness, we violate the sacred without imagining any offense, we find our wit and skill to be good for nothing. We have not encountered reality simply, rather we have encountered a reality, another reality, another mask or face of what we may never see face to face or all at once. We know better, it would seem, that and what we have failed hitherto to grasp.

We may perhaps speak of stages in this resistance. First, there is the haunting sense of something missing, a sense of deep incompleteness and lack to which nothing imaginable seems to correspond. Second, there is a glimpse of what or at least of the sort of thing we have lost. This we must learn from others, from utter strangers, for the most part. Finally, and this may be no more than a fond hope, there is the gradual regaining of our lost legacy, those insights and powers which once were but are no longer simply a part of being human. The first two of these stages seem to occur together, namely, we most often recognize that something essentially human lies outside of our experience and ken when we encounter specific ideas or actions or lives which we cannot imaginatively enter. We find human beings doing unrecognizably human things and speaking unrecognizably human truths. And yet there is a faint echo in a space within us which is hollow and uninhabited. The fit between our own cultural reality and reality itself loses its hold, the mask slips, and we grasp that there is something, something essential to our very well-being as man, that is not a portion of our inheritance here and now. We come to realize that our own familiar curriculum fails to teach us all there is to know. There are gods never mentioned in our Bibles or invoked in our churches. There are human powers we no longer dare or know how to exercise. There are sights and sounds, harmonies and tensions, to which we are simply impervious. We come to know this and more as soon as we listen to other men, not most other Americans or modern western Europeans, but utter strangers such as Tatanga Mani or Walking Buffalo who is just plain tired of our white arrogance and parochialism.

> We were lawless people, but we were on pretty good terms with the Great Spirit, creator and ruler of all. You whites assumed we were savages. You didn't understand our prayers. You didn't try to understand. When we sang our praises to the sun or moon or wind, you said we were worshipping idols. Without understanding, you condemned us as lost souls just because our form of worship was different from yours.
>
> We saw the Great Spirit's work in almost everything: sun, moon, trees, wind, and mountains. Sometimes we approached him through these things. Was that so bad? I think we have a belief in the supreme being, a stronger faith than that of most whites who have called us pagans. . . . Indians living close to nature and nature's rulers are not living in darkness.
>
> Did you know that trees talk? Well they do. They talk to each other and they'll talk to you if you listen. Trouble is, white people don't listen. They never learned to listen to the Indians so I don't suppose they'll listen to other voices in nature. But I have learned a lot from trees: sometimes about the weather, sometimes about animals, sometimes about the Great Spirit.[6]

Resistance, then, involves conversion or *metanoia*, an attending to what has been lost and yet remains always our proper possession, a turning of mind and spirit back and inward in search of itself, a metamorphosis of man from one image to another and back again. We may find one striking example of the spirit and character of resistance in the work of an otherwise less than exemplary fellow, Niccolo Machiavelli. Machiavelli saw his people accepting the heels of emperors, clerics, and princes, committed to impotence, resigned to violation. He attributed their emasculation in part to their faith, whether devout or indolent, in the Christian image of man which celebrated humility, sacrifice, and service, while uprooting the ancient virtues which had once reared and sustained the Roman republic. His writings recall his countrymen to their lost virtue; and thus he closes his famous *Prince* with a clarion call borrowed from Petrarch: "Virtue will take up arms against the fury / And the battle will be brief / For the ancient valor / Is not yet dead in Italian hearts."[7] In fact, Machiavelli claims that the peculiar diminishment and degeneration of his people is due

> not so much to the weak state to which the religion of today has brought the world, or to the evil wrought in many provinces and cities of Christendom by ambition conjoined with idleness, as to the lack of a proper appreciation of history, owing to people failing to realize the significance of what they read, and to their having no taste for the delicacies it comprises. Hence it comes about that the great bulk of those who read it take pleasure in hearing of the various incidents which are contained in it, but never think of imitating them, since they hold them to be not merely difficult but impossible of imitation, as if the heaven, the sun, the elements and man had in their motion, their order, and their potency become different from what they used to be.[8]

It is through the study of history that one learns the possible meanings of resistance, namely, that one learns of the somehow more and other than one has ever or at least of late thought oneself possibly to be. History and resistance call upon us to encounter the other and the strange not as curiosities or as threats but as possibilities which admit of and invite imitation and appropriation. We are called from one cave to the next in search of the light of day which has at one time or another lit each cave's fire, focused through a lens and brought to a moment's blaze. Education in resistance is, then, an education in history and it would seem that no culture or program of education has ever been so widely and restlessly historical as our own, which is what Nietzsche suggests and reflects upon so inimitably in his essay "The Use and Abuse of History."

> Let me give a picture of the spiritual events in the soul of the modern man. Historical knowledge streams on him from sources that are inexhaustible, strange incoherencies come together, mem-

> ory opens all its gates and yet is never open wide enough, nature busies herself to receive all the foreign guests, to honour them and put them in their places. But they are at war with each other: violent measures seem necessary, in order to escape destruction of one's self. It becomes second nature to grow gradually accustomed to this irregular and stormy homelife, though this second nature is unquestionably weaker, more restless, more radically unsound than the first. The modern man carries inside him an enormous heap of indigestible knowledge stones that occasionally rattle together in his body, as the fairy tale has it. And the rattle reveals the most striking characteristic of these modern men, the opposition of something inside them to which nothing external corresponds; and the reverse. The ancient nations knew nothing of this. Knowledge, taken in excess without hunger, even contrary to desire, has no more the effect of transforming the external life; and remains hidden in a chaotic inner world that the modern man has a curious pride in calling his "real personality." He has the substance, he says, and only wants the form; but this is quite an unreal opposition in a living thing. Our modern culture is for that reason not a living one, because it cannot be understood without that opposition. . . . For we moderns have nothing of our own. We only become worth notice by filling ourselves to overflowing with foreign customs, arts, philosophies, religions and sciences: we are wandering encyclopaedias, as an ancient Greek who had strayed into our time would probably call us. But the only value of an encyclopaedia lies in the inside, in the contents, not in what is written outside, in the binding or the wrapper. And so the whole of modern culture is essentially internal; the bookbinder prints something like this on the cover: "Manual of internal culture for external barbarians."[9]

Our education too often represents rampant, intellectual tourism. There is no genuine encounter with otherness both because of the sheer kaleidoscopic pace of one's studies and because there is no coherent vision of the world or image of man whose integrity is shocked and challenged by what we encounter elsewhere. History must be a dialogue, passionate and sustained, which it is not for us, because we fail to listen and because we have nothing to say. Rather, we record; but for whom? Spelunkers, not at heart but by profession, we deal in caves like real-estate brokers who "show" homes but seem not to live anywhere or, to borrow an image from Kierkegaard, we deal in ideas with all of the slick savoir faire of a garment salesman. Perhaps the saddest and most telling comment on our modern character is made by T. S. Eliot in his little-known work *After Strange Gods* when he says that we live in a society which has for the most part ceased to be capable of exercising blasphemy or of recognizing it. Without the capacity for blasphemy there is no faith to affirm or to deny, no perfection to pursue or to flee. Again in Nietzsche's words:

> All living things need an atmosphere, a mysterious mist, around them. If that veil be taken away and a religion, an art, or a genius condemned to revolve like a star without an atmosphere, we must not be surprised if it becomes hard and unfruitful, and soon withers. . . .
>
> Every people, every man even, who would become ripe, needs such a veil of illusion, such a protecting cloud. But now men hate to become ripe, for they honor history above life.[10]

The name for our present condition is pluralism, which aspires to resistance all at once without pain, without conflict, without growth. What the resulting synthetic harmony exacts from its adherents is a fundamental disinterestedness, a severely ascetic self-denial or self-diminishment for the sake of denying nothing, excluding nothing. The tragedy is that neither is anything affirmed or cherished or nurtured to full growth. The student of history is presented with a gamut of despair, a vast series of opposing claims and possibilities which are known only so far as to be named and stationed correctly as terms in a quadratic equation of sorts which cancels perfectly in the end, one hopes at graduation, without remainder, with no remaining unknowns. The standard curricular course of study recalls a child's dot-puzzle in which the child pushes his pencil from dot to dot in numbered sequence only to find a picture emerge in the end. As one grows older one has to pass through fewer dots before the hidden image emerges. Then one day one is too old for such games as one sees the image at once. The same is true of modern education. The courses or subjects for study are not studied for their own sakes as worlds in which one might wish to dwell for a while or forever but as points to be passed through and accumulated so as to furnish the student sooner or later with the one critical and fundamentally cynical insight required to live at peace in a pluralistic society, the insight which Descartes drew from his own privileged education, namely, that there is no such thing as the wisdom he once sought.

Thought and reflection can bring us no further than this point, can do no more than suggest the infinite, unresolvable multiplicity of opinion and thus suggest the practical primacy of one's own opinions and those of one's times and of skillfully suiting the one to the other. It is no wonder that the characteristic college graduate wants nothing so desperately as to engage in work, manual or at least practical, uncritically and wordlessly. The modern study of history is, by design and by default, a gamut of despair in which young minds are tooled down for a mindless age, a gamut of despair which Nietzsche characterized as follows:

> The young man is kicked through all the centuries: boys who know nothing of war, diplomacy, or commerce are considered fit to be introduced to political history. We moderns also run through art galleries and hear concerts in the same way as the young man runs through history. We can feel that one thing sounds differently from another, and pronounce on the different "effects." And the power of gradually losing all feelings of strangeness or astonishment, and finally being pleased at anything, is called the historical sense, or historical culture. The crowd of influences streaming on the young soul is so great, the clods of barbarism and violence flung at him so strange and overwhelming, that an assumed stupidity is his only refuge. Where there is a subtler and stronger self-consciousness we find another emotion too—disgust. The young man has become homeless: he doubts all ideas, all moralities. He knows "it was different in every age, and what you are does not matter." In a heavy apathy he lets opinion on opinion pass by him, and understands the meaning of Hölderlin's words when he read the work of Diogenes Laertius on the lives and doctrines of the Greek philosophers: "I have seen here too what has often occurred to me, that the change and waste in men's thoughts and systems is far more tragic than the fates that overtake what men are accustomed to call the only realities." No, such study of history bewilders and overwhelms. It is not necessary for youth, as the ancients show, but even in the highest degree dangerous, as the moderns show. Consider the historical student, the heir of ennui, that appears even in his boyhood. He has the "methods" for original work, the "correct ideas" and the

> airs of the master at his fingers' ends. A little isolated period of the past is marked out for sacrifice. He cleverly applies his method, and produces something, or rather, in prouder phrase, "creates" something. He becomes a "servant of truth" and a ruler in the great domain of history. If he was what they call ripe as a boy, he is now over-ripe. You only need shake him and wisdom will rattle down into your lap; but the wisdom is rotten, and every apple has its worm.[11]

Resistance, we have said, is a matter of conversion, conversion to the fullness of one's own human possibilities. Recalling Francis Bacon's stunning word for the same marvelous turning which he hoped for in his own time, resistance is a matter of "instauration," a making all things new again as they have always somehow been. Surely this will never be the aim or the accomplishment of formal education, programmed and accredited. But is it possible at all, anywhere or ever? I know of no more profound consideration of or response to this question than that of Sophocles in his drama *Philoctetes*[12]; and I would know of no finer way to draw our own reflections on resistance towards a provisional close than to meditate upon the words of Sophocles regarding resistance and conversion. It is clearly the play of a very old man on the verge of childhood, a play which thinks new and old thoughts at once. As such the play is divided between young Neoptolemus and old Philoctetes and tells of their friendship. But our meditation now requires a scene to be sketched and inhabited before we can dwell therein.

The place is Lemnos, an island in the North Aegean Sea west of Troy where a seemingly endless seige continues to the decimation of Greeks and Trojans alike. Recently, Helenus, son of Priam and prophet, a captive of Odysseus, has prophesied that the Greeks will never take Troy without Philoctetes and his divine bow, a gift of friendship from Heracles. But Philoctetes has long since been marooned on Lemnos, abandoned by Odysseus who could not tolerate the stench and the groans of an old man with a festering foot cursed for treading unknowingly on a sacred grove. Philoctetes props himself upon his bow and clings to his humanity. We must recall that, for the Greeks, to cease to exist before the eyes and ears of others, in public space—the assembly, the athletic field, the battleground and finally the memory of one's city—was to fail or to cease to exist at all as a full human being. Thus the exile of Philoctetes has threatened to obscure and diminish his humanity just as his cancerous foot lunges at him, dragging him to his knees and to his hands, down from the posture of a man to that of a beast. It is his bow, the token of a distant divine friendship, the recollection of an act of compassion recognized and rewarded by Heracles, which sustains the weight of his oppressed humanity. He enters the play in a state of existential tension, half-man and half-beast, like the centaur in whose blood his fatal arrows had once been dipped. One day he too must die, fall from his feet and die on the ground like any beast must. For the moment, he lives and clings to his humanity, his posture, his wits, his honor. In telling young Neoptolemus of his burden and sickness he will say "Terrible it is, beyond word's reach. But pity me," and of his hopes for deliverance he will add "an empty prayer, I am afraid, boy . . . I look for something new."

Neoptolemus too is poised in tension between humanity and inhumanity. He is a boy only half-grown, away from the sheltered denying obscurity of his home for the first time. In terms of our earlier discussion he is for Odysseus still a young boy in his keep, subject to him, to be moved at will; but Philoctetes alone recognizes that Neoptolemus is coming of age. He sees in him the image, the recollection of Neoptolemus' dead father, Achilles, and draws Neoptolemus into full posture as the grown son of a great man, the heir to a hero whose blood mixes with his own. Neoptolemus is brought along by Odysseus to deceive Philoctetes who would surely listen to innocent assurances from a nobly born boy and who would just as surely never listen to the jagged wiles of infamous Odysseus. Neoptolemus is simply in Odysseus' command, a boy used to being commanded and moved not unlike a slave within his own home, and he merely asks of Odysseus "tell me what you want." Odysseus cautions him to "be loyal" and adds:

> If you should hear
> some strange new thing, unlike what you have heard
> before, still serve us; it was to serve you came here.

A wily and powerful expression of *apaideusia*, the attempt to stay resistance, to control the future of the slavish child within familiar slavish bounds. Neoptolemus is urged to ignore and refuse anything strange, anything new, which he might encounter. Odysseus admits that such a command is likely to press against Neoptolemus' "natural bent" and offers a further assurance:

> Bear up: another time we shall prove honest.
> For one brief shameless portion of a day
> give me yourself, and then for all the rest
> you may be called most scrupulous of men.

Odysseus knows the force of habit, the weight that one brief shameless portion of a day will place upon the next such portion, and asks for one moment's service at a time. Within the soul of Neoptolemus there rages a searing conflict between his "natural antipathy to get [his] ends by tricks and stratagem," and the fact, as he admits it to Odysseus, "that I was sent with you to follow your instructions." Finally, the chorus knows that the tension will blaze forth and require to be resolved. There will be no avoiding the strange and the new; for, as they say, "we are strangers, and the land is strange." What follows is a meeting, of souls and hearts and hopes, of the old Philoctetes, grown a savage, and the young Neoptolemus, still a boy. Only the untrammeled, unknowing Neoptolemus is able to lead Philoctetes from his cave where he fled from the guile and ravaging of Odysseus and men like him. And only the knowing, broken Philoctetes is able to lead Neoptolemus from his boyish servitude to the whims of his keepers. What follows, simply, is friendship. Neoptolemus enters Philoctetes' cave, stays with him through his cursed seizure, and lifts him to his feet, restoring him to the trust and love which is human fellowship. To recall the beautiful words of a beautiful friend, Philoctetes learns once again the simple human truth that "the reason why men have arms is not in order to ward off, but in order to embrace."[13] And yet this is too simple. Friendship too must be exposed to the public realm where Philoctetes has seen that nothing evil perishes and nothing good is spared by the Gods who must be evil. He must endure still another deception, still another curse.

The young Neoptolemus is not simply unknowing, not without guile. The father of his soul is not the father of his blood; Philoctetes looked at him and saw the image of Achilles whereas he should have looked and now must look at him and see the image of Odysseus.

In fact, Neoptolemus is poised between the two. Only one shameful portion of a day has passed of his new age. He has only once exercised his freedom and acted among men; and his act was one of deception and betrayal. He does not know what to say; at a loss for words, he explains "all is disgust when one leaves his own nature and does things that misfit it." Philoctetes despairs once again of others' and of his own humanity, and with a mad torrent of outrage, perhaps not heard again until Shakespeare's Lear, calls upon the powers and beings of nature for a hearing:

> Caverns and headlands, dens of wild creatures,
> you jutting broken crags, to you I raise my cry—
> there is no one else that I can speak to—

But he does finally turn to Neoptolemus, looking one last time for something new.

> Be your true self again. Will you not?
> No word. Then I am nothing.

Philoctetes continues to articulate a theory of resistance, conversion, and renewal whose truth only Neoptolemus can prove to them both by acting afresh, acting beyond the shame and gravity of one moment and seizing his lost youth again. "You are not bad yourself; by bad men's teaching you came to practice your foul lesson. . . . Are we slaves and not free? Is it as such our fathers have begotten us?" Only Neoptolemus will respond to this. In fact he has two fathers or more, as we all do. For now betrayed by others and by himself, he is learning what Philoctetes said he learned from his cursed disease and disgust:

> Necessity has taught me,
> little by little, to suffer and be patient.

Finally Neoptolemus, the new warrior, the young warrior, stands as a man, sprung from a noble father, and takes up again, receives anew, his freedom to act. He embodies, personifies, speaks out the possibility of resistance, the reality of the new and the strange. Freedom and spontaneity, once lost, once impaired, are restored. His words are direct and powerful like arrows launched from a tall and seasoned bow: "I go to undo the wrong that I have done." To Odysseus he is still a boy doing something characteristically rash. "Nothing rash," answers Neoptolemus. "I am going to give something back. . . . It was a sin, a shameful sin, which I shall try to retrieve." Once again Philoctetes must be beckoned from his cave, schooled again in the possibility of humanity outside of caves. Once convinced of innocence he must now be convinced of forgiveness. He fears, and Neoptolemus asks: "Is there no place, then, for repentance?" Philoctetes responds with a curse:

> You will say it all
> to no purpose for you will never win my heart
> to friendship with you, who have stolen my life
> by treachery, and then came and preached to me,
> bad son of a noble father. Cursed be you all,
> first the two sons of Atreus, then Odysseus,
> and then yourself!

Freedom and trust, once lost, may, it seems, never be regained. We seem free only once and in fact never know true freedom. For we are old before we are young. We are all wicked sons and daughters of noble stock, miseducated by "shabby slit-eyed souls" who like us themselves became old too soon. So it would seem to be were it not for the final new and strange thing, the *daimōn* of the gods.

It is Heracles alone who is able to restore the friendship of Philoctetes and Neoptolemus and thus allow them to leave their inhuman cavelike existences and share a common island in fellowship. It is Heracles who in the end must speak, the bestower of the divine bow of friendship and it is for Philoctetes to say simply, "I shall not disobey," and for Neoptolemus to add, "Nor I." It is a great destiny (*megalē Moira*), an all-overpowering divine presence and power (*pandamator daimōn*), a mysterious source of renewal and resolve, simply to be reverenced and to be obeyed, which finally grounds the hope of resistance.[14] Both Neoptolemus and Philoctetes were able, each in his own privileged time, to dream and to speak of the new and the strange and of the lost and the marooned; but finally neither was able to grasp it except in response to a power and a presence which he had to await in patience and suffering. So it seems to be with resistance and renewal. Zarathustra speaks of three metamorphoses of spirit which bear some resemblance to the three stages of resistance: "the spirit becomes a camel; and the camel, a lion; and the lion, finally a child."[15] We are capable of and perhaps know the reverent spirit and the eventually hollow desolation of the pack animal burdened with a past that is not fully our own and to which we cannot simply belong. Some of us may even muster up the rage of the lion casting off the limits and the slavish weight of the "thou shalt." But it is not for us to be reborn from ourselves and with Nicodemus we feel foolish in asking if we must enter the womb twice over. "The child is innocence and forgetting, a new game, a self-propelled wheel, a first movement, a sacred 'Yes.' "[16] In reflecting upon what we have lost and in searching thus for the new and the strange, our journey will be one of thought and speech. As such we shall never be children. But we may hope for and trust in a great destiny, an all-subduing demon, not Descartes' demon of deception but a demon who will reward our patience and our reverence and allow us to speak these words one day from the heart:

> By the great mercies
> I have been returned to the sources of power
> to live there by the flames dancing on their bed of coal
> the water jetting from its hole in the rock
> alive the elements,
> and we
> neither soused nor burned
> by the great mercies
> have returned.[17]

NOTES

1. Aristotle *Rhetoric* 1. 10. 1370a6–8, trans. Richard McKeon, in *Collected Works* (New York: Random House, 1941).

2. *I Have Spoken*, ed. Virginia Irving Armstrong (Chicago: Swallow, 1971), pp. 16–17.

3. My use of the term "resistance" throughout this chapter is prompted and illuminated by a splendid essay by D. S. Carne-Ross entitled "The Arts of Resistance." Anything which I am able to say regarding this question will be deepened and clarified by a reading of Carne-Ross's essay. See *Toothing Stones: Rethinking the Political*, ed. Robert E. Meagher (Chicago: Swallow, 1972), pp. 223ff.

4. Cf. Aristotle *On the Soul* 3. 7. 431a17–18, 431b3–4, 432a8–9; *Metaphysics* 4. 6. 1011b26–28.

5. I am indebted to my friend William Walsh O'Grady who pointed out the relation between this biblical account and Socratic refutation in a marvelous lecture essay entitled "The Search for Common Objects."

6. *Touch the Earth*, ed. T. C. McLuhan (New York: Simon & Schuster, 1972), p. 23. Copyright © 1971 by T. C. McLuhan. Reprinted by permission of Dutton-Sunrise, Inc., a subsidiary of E. P. Dutton & Co., Inc.

7. Niccolo Machiavelli, *The Prince*, trans. A. Robert Caponigri (Chicago: Henery Regnery Co., 1963), p. 134.

8. Niccolo Machiavelli, *The Discourses*, trans. Leslie J. Walker, S.J., ed. Bernard Grick (Baltimore: Penguin, 1970), pp. 98–99.

9. Friedrich Nietzsche, *The Use and Abuse of History*, trans. Adrian Collins (Indianapolis: Bobbs-Merrill, 1957), pp. 23–24. Copyright © 1949, 1957 by The Liberal Arts Press, Inc. Reprinted by permission of The Bobbs-Merrill Company, Inc.

10. Ibid., p. 44.

11. Ibid., pp. 45–46.

12. The translation which I shall refer to in the passages cited in my discussion of the *Philoctetes* is by David Grene (University of Chicago Press, 1957).

13. From commencement remarks to the Class of 1974 of St. John's College, Annapolis, Md., by William Walsh O'Grady, tutor.

14. I have learned much from and done only slim justice to William Walsh O'Grady's insights into the *Philoctetes* to be found in an unpublished essay on the meaning of *analabein* and *daimon* in this play.

15. Friedrich Nietzsche, *Thus Spake Zarathustra*, pt. 1, in *The Portable Nietzsche*, trans. Walter Kaufmann (New York: Viking Press, 1954), p. 137.

16. Ibid., p. 139.

17. "Runes," an as yet unpublished poem by Elizabeth Sewell.

> The Ruler of all, as a man proposing games, or giving a banquet and being about to invite others to feast and to behold the spectacle, first provided everything for every kind of entertainment, in order that when man came into the world he might at once find a feast ready for him, and a most holy theatre.
>
> Philo Judaeus

CHAPTER FOUR

SEEING

What we begin here may be thought of as an exercise book in resistance, inescapably self-conscious resistance and, for that reason, perhaps self-defeating resistance. But we cannot be other than altogether self-conscious when, like young Neoptolemus, it is our lot to confront a lost youthfulness, a lost freedom and freshness of action and thought, and so to take up, receive again, and give back what was taken and lost from our shared lives. As such, we may think of this work as the compiling of a primer in philosophy, a first book in philosophy which is fatefully aware that

> Before philosophizing one must live; and life demands that we put on blinders, that we look neither to the right nor to the left nor behind us, but straight ahead in the direction we have to go. Our knowledge, far from being made up of a gradual association of simple elements, is the effect of a sudden dissociation: from the immensely vast field of our virtual knowledge, we have selected, in order to make it into actual knowledge, everything which concerns our actions upon things; we have neglected the rest. . . .
>
> Would not the role of philosophy under such circumstances be to lead us to a complete perception of reality by means of a certain displacement of our attention? It would be a question of *turning* this attention *aside* from the part of the universe which interests us from a practical viewpoint and *turning* it *back* toward what serves no practical purpose. This conversion of attention would be philosophy itself.[1]

In short, we must learn to see again, not from an already familiar, convenient, self-serving perspective upon objects likewise familiar and indebted to that attention of ours. Rather, we must learn to see again for the full joy of seeing and thus seek out those objects which will fill our eyes, the eyes of our body and the eyes of our soul, to overflowing. And so we must be willing to look upon the as yet unseen in a light or a darkness (we have found the two to be experientially interchangeable) to which our eyes are quite unaccustomed. We quit our own familiar haunts to enter the subterranean search for the light of day. In the beginning we must be willing to dwell in caves other than our own; and it may be that we are capable of no more than an honest beginning or a series of beginnings, left only to imagine what completion and wholeness of vision might be like. And yet each cave, each spiritual *polis*, hewn quickly and haphazardly in moments of daimonic presence and power from the solid rock of human resistance to the truth, each such cave preserves wonders commonplace to their heirs and strange to others like ourselves.

Such wonders—sometimes curious, sometimes shocking, sometimes incomprehensibly engaging—offer us a share in that wonder with which all philosophy and all wisdom begin. And there are moments when to begin seems to be not only enough but all that we can stand. For our many descendings into the Hades of the seemingly invisible (Plato frequently puns on "Hades" which is so close to the Greek word for invisible), we shall require guides whose eyes are keener and more widely and deeply schooled, which in the Greek would mean leisured, than our own. And our first such guide will be Leonardo da Vinci who looked upon nature as a secret which discloses itself unendingly to the inquiring eye. His notebooks tell of an insatiably curious and appreciative see-er who looked not only into the present appearances of the world but peered as well into the past through the traces and fossiled recollections of the past to be found in caves. Leonardo's own account of his exploration of one such cave may provide us with an image, an imaginative glimpse, of our own acts of resistance, historical inquiry, and philosophy—all three a single work ensouled with a common longing for the light of day for which we must paradoxically wander through subterranean worlds.

> Impelled by an ungovernable longing to behold the vast abundance of the varied and strange forms that nature has created . . . I came to the entrance of a large cave. Bending my back, my left hand clutching my knee and with my right shading my lowered, contracted eyebrows, I peered to see if there was anything to be distinguished, but the deep darkness impeded my view. After I had been there for some time, two feelings stirred within me: dread of the gloomy, menacing cave and desire to find out whether there was anything marvellous in it.[2]

When we speak of seeing we have in mind a range of possibilities barely suggested by the mere perception of colors and shapes. And yet the sight of reds and blues and circles and lines already introduces us to the world of seeing which we wish to explore. By seeing we are to have in mind a particular image of man in the face of which one's mind might first open and one's heart first leap towards a spectrum of possibilities encompassing the smear of color before an infant's undiscerning eyes and, at the same time, the contemplative's sightless beholding of the invisible sun of being. From the one to the other, from the undisciplined eye of the child to the inner eye of the most truthful soul, there is a straight line, an unfolding spectrum of possibilities, so akin to and inseparable from one another that they must be thought of and spoken of under the same image, the same metaphor, of seeing. They belong to a common world and Plato places them along a single line, divided into distinct sections, but nonetheless a single line, unbroken and continuous. Our reflections upon seeing will then pass along this line, ascending from sensory sight to spiritual sight, from sight to insight and contemplation.

It will be indeed inescapable that we shall speak of inner and outer, of sense and of spirit, mirrored in a common image; and yet we must and shall endeavor to glimpse the wholeness and oneness of being and thus of our beholding of being. For there is no thinking for man so theoretical, so far from the outer world of sense, that it does not have its own peculiar color and shape; and there is no sensing for man so immediate, so far from the world of thought, that it is void of memory and considerations of form. The eyes of the body and the eyes of the soul dwell together as do their proper objects in the world. In short, man is embodied and soulful; and for him, both pure thought and pure matter are sheer hypotheses, imaginative abstractions from all that he is given and from all that he knows straight on. There is no inclination of the mind that is not at the same time a posture of the body—the possibilities of the one are always somehow the possibilities of the other, more or less refined, more or less perfect. For now, then, we shall consider the peculiar character and perfection of seeing and thus the possibilities of man as a see-er.

With a view towards the full range of seeing from perception (*aisthēsis*) to contemplation (*theōria*), and of their appropriate unity, I wish to begin these reflections upon seeing with a rather simple parable first told by Pythagoras. It seems[3] that Pythagoras once came to Phlius and entered into discussions with Leon, the ruler of the Phlians. Now Pythagoras was the first man to speak of himself as a "philosopher" and it was on this curious new name and art that Leon's interests were focused. Wondering at the gifts of Pythagoras, Leon asked him to name the art in which he most deeply placed his trust. Pythagoras replied that he was skilled in no particular art but that, rather, he was a philosopher. Then tell me, Leon asked further, who these philosophers are and how they differ from the rest of men. In response, Pythagoras told this parable which I shall translate rather freely from the account by Pythagoras' biographer, Iamblichus.[4] Surely there were philosophers before they were named such, but the moment of naming a person, an activity, a life, or even a god, or of receiving their names, is a privileged moment when the reality of what is now with name shines forth with a clarity and a freshness perhaps never before attained and perhaps soon lost. The act of naming is an act of disclosure, an act of insight and of the sharing of insight. And here the insight is into sight itself, a seeing of seeing. The peculiar possibility of seeing, culminating in the seeing of the philosopher, here comes to self-consciousness and to self-expression in an originally quite simple manner. Such a moment and its story are privileged and are to be recalled whenever we strive to regain and restore what they testify to.

> The paths men take with their lives remind me of the various ways men take part in the Olympic games.
>
> No one comes year after year without something in mind, something to be gained, something to be enjoyed. There are the merchants who set up stands for their wares, driving a hard bargain and pushing for steep profits. Then there are the athletes who display the disciplined powers of their bodies in the hope of applause and fame. Finally there is a third kind (*eidos*) of person who, with a freedom surpassing all others, takes in all the customary wonders of the festival—the fine craftworks, the shining feats of the athletes, and the exquisite lines of the poets—all for the joy of the beholding.
>
> In the same ways do diverse men gather together in life, rivalling one another, each in pursuit of his own delights. Some men are driven by the lust for money and for the luxuries which money can afford. Others fill their hearts with strife and frenzy in their mad pursuit of glory, supremacy, and rule. But again there is a third type (*tropos*) of man, the purest of all, who desires nothing more or other than the simple beholding of the loveliest things. And this is the kind of man whom we call a philosopher.

Pythagoras goes on to say what sort of things the loveliest or fairest things might be which are the proper and distinguishing objects of the philosopher's gaze; for the man or kind of man whom Pythagoras calls a philosopher is not unique in his capacity for sight. The merchant surely has an eye for fabrics or metals and the athlete has as keen an eye for the mark he must reach or strike. Rather, the philosopher is distinguished by his single-minded and wholehearted attention to seeing, to the perfection of his own capacity for sight and to the seeking out of its purest, most appropriate objects which Pythagoras describes as those beautiful things which are first and divine and undying and ever self-sustaining. Philosophy, he says, is the zealous pursuit of "this kind of sight," a sight whose preeminence and perfection is derived from its objects rather than from any willfully assumed perspective or state of mind which might be brought to these or to any other objects. Consequently, we may not speak of sight apart from peculiar sights; and *paideia*, the education of men as see-ers, will involve an inquiry into the most appropriate objects of human seeing as well as the endeavor to render men well-suited to the vision of those objects. Such an inquiry as that, or as this one, would do well, it would seem, to begin with the simplest objects of sight and the simplest elements of those objects.

In reflecting upon vision and the visual world it is reasonable that we should seek out and accept the counsel of the painter, the visual artist, who presumably attends with special care and sensitivity to the nature of seeing and of sights and who may then be able to set us on our way with some knowing assurance of the path to be taken. For now we are putting to ourselves a simple question: What are the simplest elements of the visible? Leonardo, in his *Treatise on Painting*,[5] lists the first principles of the science of painting as follows: the point, the line, the surface, and then the body bounded by a given surface. These principles would seem likewise to describe with simple clarity the essential elements of the visible, the necessary and sufficient conditions for anything at all to be seen. If anything is to present itself to our eyes, it must be extended in space before us within a finite visual field. We cannot see what is without spatial extension and what is without appropriate limits to its spatial extension. Whatever else, then, might be true to say of a given visible object, it is surely extended within the space before us if it is seen or to be seen at all.

It is critical in this discussion that we have in mind the simplest of visual objects, say, a line or a number of lines, which, however, neither picture nor symbolize anything else. For the moment we introduce images, much less words, or even objects whose names we know or which we know must have names, we are already well beyond mere sight, mere visual perception. In fact, honesty demands that we recognize ourselves to be simply unable to isolate the experience of vision from thinking, much less from the other senses. We cannot truthfully think of ourselves as see-ers alone, any more than we may think of any visual object as see-able alone. And yet there are moments when the experience of vision seems to surpass, to exclude, and to suffice for all other experiences just as there are objects of sight so distant, so silent, and so brilliant that to see them seems to be all that is possible and seems to be enough. And our present exercise of focusing on sight alone and on the simplest of sights so as to discern in the most elementary of ways the nature of seeing, has finally as its aim to understand such moments of full vision.

The world of sight is immersed in time and yet remains somehow timeless. There is surely motion and change among the objects of sight and there is motion and change within the very act of seeing. And yet there is a dialectic of the timeful and the timeless which is peculiar to the world and to the act of sight. As I open my eyes again from a night's sleep or from a moment's passion or pain, the world awaits my eyes seemingly as it has always been and surely not allowing the illusion that what I see is a simple creation of my eyes. The same would seem to be even more dramatically the case when I open my eyes for the very first time; and while we have no simple reflective access to such an experience, Schopenhauer, citing a medical study by Gilbert, interestingly notes that "blind persons operated on behold the first light with great joy."[6] Furthermore, we first see for the most part all at once. At each moment, as I open my eyes, before I am able to focus upon anything in particular, I am always first presented with a whole which I seem not to take any time to see. "We know clearly that vision is one of the swiftest actions there is," explains Leonardo, "and in an instant sees infinite forms; nevertheless, it understands only one thing at a time." Thus, in the next moment of sight, the whole is lost to me and the original whole becomes a frame within which I begin to focus first upon this part and now upon that part. This sequence may be repeated if only I again close my eyes and open them naïvely, not willfully, not determined to focus at once on a particular sight which I have previously located and singled out for immediate attention. I seem not to be able to reconstruct or to restore the lost wholeness for myself; rather, it remains a gift like the very light itself from out of the darkness into which I necessarily, sometimes voluntarily and sometimes involuntarily, lapse.

Even though our first experience of sight or each first experience of sight is somehow *of* the whole, it is not itself whole but partial, flawed, and unsatisfying. And there ensues our own endeavor to complete and to perfect our sight of the whole by regaining it, comprehending it bit by bit. We study it with care, discursively, allowing our gaze to pass over it, to range across it, focusing first here, then there. Our aim in this activity is to see the whole again, this time wholly. And yet, as we have already seen, the whole must be given to us anew not as the product of our analytic and synthetic efforts but as a pure and timeless gift. Seeing, then, discursive and scanning, occurs in time and takes time and yet serves only to articulate and to understand what was and is fully present, in its wholeness and in its particularity, to one's first glance and remains present throughout one's deliberate successive glances. In short, the see-er discovers his world, a whole, always already there, complete and perfect and copresent with him. And what requires to be completed is the see-er's vision of that whole by his own articulation of that whole to himself through a series of intentional, focused glances and by the light's fresh bestowal of the whole upon him, freely and graciously.

I do not wish to deny or to overlook that there are some sights which simply cannot be seen all at once or which are never simply or enduringly available to us as see-ers. With respect to the latter, there are, to be sure, events in the visual world, so eventfully unpredictable and sudden, that we seem barely to see them at all, for example a comet's streaking fire or lightning's flash. Most sights, however, both because of the impressive span of our own visual field and because of our own mobility present themselves to us as objects which leave us free to see them, to close our eyes, to turn away, to refocus, and to return to them, namely as objects copresent with us as see-ers. Furthermore, most sights admit of being seen at once whole, never wholly or perfectly, but somehow all at once. Admittedly, there are occasional ambiguities in our sight from the beginning and the ambiguities increase in number and depth as soon as we are concerned to "read" our sights, to name what we see, namely, to interpret or to think as we see. And it may be claimed that this concern never leaves us.

Artists often consciously introduce time into the sights which they create, presenting us with an object so timeful, namely, so visually ambiguous or circuitous that it simply cannot be seen all at once. For example, once we become aware of the essential ambiguity of the two pictures presented below, that is, once we see that the rabbit may be read as a duck or the duck as a rabbit and that the zigzagging band of rectangles may be read as starting either from behind or from the front, our eyes cannot seem to settle on one or other reading for longer than a moment, when we are forcibly, as it were, distracted by and drawn back and then forth between the two.

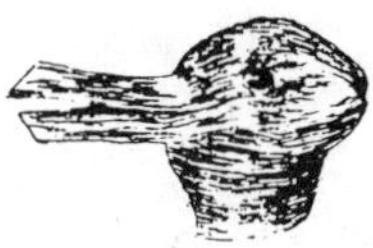

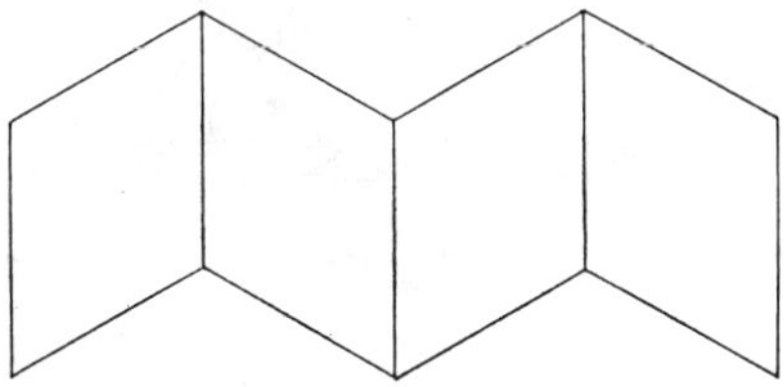

Or we will inevitably fall into asking, with this sketch, which hand is drawing which—an obviously endless question.

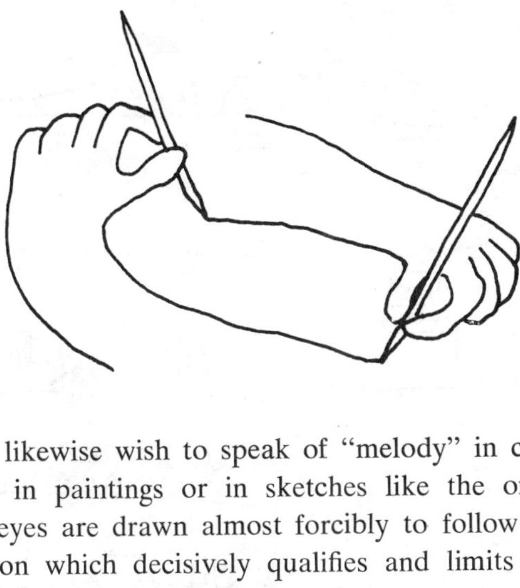

We may likewise wish to speak of "melody" in certain sights, particularly in paintings or in sketches like the one below, in which our eyes are drawn almost forcibly to follow a prescribed line of vision which decisively qualifies and limits the freedom and spontaneity of focus peculiar to seeing.

Most all of these exceptions, however, belong to the realm of what may be called visual thinking or a seeking which seeks to read, interpret, or name its sights as images not simply to be seen but

somehow to be seen through. Sight, as opposed to insight, which is inevitably and notably purposeful and discursive in its movements if not in its moments of repose, is remarkably timeless and, as we shall now discuss briefly, remarkably free.

Once our eyes open to a world which presents itself to them in the full light of day, they range freely across the whole at their own initiative and pace. No one beginning finally excludes another: for a moment's respite, a moment's retreat into darkness, is all that is required for a fresh beginning. Admittedly, after some time, seeing is quite subject to habituation so that one sees mostly what one is predisposed to see, in precisely the order and the mode of one's earlier experiences. And there are sights which even at first sight attract our gaze, forcibly and possessively, holding it still and rapt in vision of them. Nevertheless, if we cling to the experience, perhaps partially the hypothesis, of pure or fresh sight, we notice that our sight proceeds noncommittally within the visible whole, leaving us free as we have always been and leaving that whole free as it has always been. The beholder and the beheld let each other be; and both remain free from and for each other. "Neither invades the sphere of the other; they let each other be what and as they are, and thus emerge the self-contained object and the self-contained subject."[7] We are "engaged," but never against our will and never overpoweringly. Rather, we are filled with our seeing precisely as and insofar as we freely open ourselves to sights which disclose themselves to us with a corresponding freedom. Our posture is one of weakness and availability as we stand before what is likewise weak and available. Neither asserts or withholds itself; rather, both are simply present to and for each other. And thus as we close our eyes or as the sun sets, all is as it was, untrammeled, nothing done, nothing undone. Still, it is not as if nothing has occurred; for there is recollection, which retains the seeing and the seen in their togetherness and in their mutual fulfillment. Nevertheless, seeing is always properly present with a view towards nothing else, nothing past or future, nothing outside the field of vision in which the seeing occurs and is engaged. It is pleasant but unprofitable; there is, in sight, a frequent overflowing and excess but always without remainder.

The experience of vision is always an experience of what is both "other" and "common." Vision is essentially "ecstatic"—a standing beyond what is simply private and unique to the individual seer and a standing within what is public and shareable with others. The experience of vision is always a communing in what is commonly accessible to all those who have not been deprived of their sight from birth, by accident, or by choice and habit. Thus, despite the numerous instances of absent, imperfect, and deluded sight—all providing ample hypothetical grounds for calling into question and doubt any single instance of sight—the experience of seeing carries with it an immediate assurance of the existence of the seen object just as the experience of thinking carries with it an immediate assurance of the existence of the thinking subject. Sight carries with it a natural assurance and trust that what is seen is indeed "there," not uniquely there for me, but there quite simply, for anyone at all to see who has eyes to see. True enough, some men are blind from birth, others have been losing their sight apace ever since; then there are any number of tricks in the world of sight. In short, our capacity for sight represents a vast spectrum exercised from an infinite variety of perspectives towards a field often impervious and unfaithful to our energies. On the face of it, it would seem that one could never assume that what is seen is seen—that you and I see the same thing when we point out something over there to each other. And yet we do go right on and assume just that. One man's sight seems quite enough to question another's inability to see and one man's inability to see seems grounds enough for his questioning another man's sight. If I see something, then I assume that it must be there to be seen. If it cannot be seen by others who are copresent with me, then my copresence with the visible is necessarily called into question. To see is always to hold what is seen at least potentially in common with others, to let something be in its universal availability. What is seen may be pointed to and spoken of with the assurance, not that what one is saying about the seen is necessarily true to it, but that one's words have a commonly accessible referent in experience and thus a readily available criterion for a debate of their truth. Without sight there could be no gathering together for open debate and resolution of our inevitable and all but intractable differences.

It is this last characteristic of sight and of sights—their "in-commonness"—that is of the most peculiar significance to us now and to our inquiry. It is this characteristic, as well, which merits for sight a preeminence over the other senses in the estimate of the Greeks who will be our guides in the world of sight so commonplace to them and so foreign to us. They speak of seeing as the purest of the senses, that which approximates most closely the realm of the immaterial and the spiritual. It would be a very great task, indeed, to trace the meaning and the relationship of the material and the spiritual in Greek literature and then to bring in our findings to inform and illumine this present discussion. Such is clearly not feasible and I will risk instead several quite ranging and perhaps precarious claims in this regard.

There is no distinction for the Greeks so pervasive and so decisive as that between the gods and men, which means that between the immortals and the mortals. Death is the divide between the mortals (the dead, the living or the not-yet-dead, the dying) and the immortals (those who will never die). To be mortal is not only, and not perhaps primarily, to be forced to endure the last pain of the moment of death; rather, to be mortal is to be forced to endure incessant diminishment and limitation, to live under the yoke of necessity (*anagkē*), the final weight or blow of which is death itself. Man must live with what is given him, his fate, poured and mixed by the gods from the twin urns of good and ill fortune, without justice and without recourse; and no man's portion is enough. His desires are restless and infinite and everything corresponding to those desires is finite. Man's frustration is deep and essential and final. His endemic quarrel with his own condition extends, as a matter of course, to others like himself with whom he is placed at odds in a struggle for what is always diminished as it is shared and for what is never enough anyway. Only in a world that simply overflows, a world free of *anagkē*, could men dwell together without designs upon one another's goods and lives. However qualified and transcended, this is the Greek perception of the most immediate and obvious look of man's fate and its consequences. These consequences were, however, altogether unacceptable for the most political of all peoples, who at the same time glimpsed the near-divinity of man.

This perception of man as simply subject to necessity and of the world as admitting only of diminishment does not allow for political life, common life, but only for tyranny, individual or collective. If it is always true that everything corresponding to our deepest desires and longings, to the ache of human insufficiency, is never enough and is always the kind of thing that what you have of it I cannot have and what I have of it you cannot have, then there is indeed an endemic war of all against all, however the lines are drawn and however many truces are designed and agreed to. Without a common good corresponding to what we most wish and need—without a good or goods which are not diminished as they are shared and without our sharing in them being able to bring a release or at least a respite from the fundamental necessity of our lives—there can be no talk or experience of political life. And in discovering and affirming political life the Greeks must have at least glimpsed and must have concerned themselves essentially with disclosing the experience of such a common good.

The experience of sensory sight suggests the reality of goods which may be shared without being diminished and the reality of our share in such goods. For a beautiful sight does not become less fully pleasant to me as I point it out and share it with you. Indeed, the reality of a beautiful sight seems to be enriched as does my sight of it even as it is shared. In fact, when I see such a sight alone I long for others to share it with and I feel my own experience of it to be somewhat diminished by their absence; and I suspect such feelings are not peculiar to myself. True enough, after a certain point, viewers get into each others' way and obstruct the view, and the view itself changes and perishes. And we long to touch, to consume, to live and not ourselves perish. Sensory sight is neither pure nor full enough to answer our deepest questions or to respond to our deepest needs or to support our common life; but its delight and freedom suggests that human *anagkē* may be less than crushing and might admit of fuller respite and joy. Finally, sight suggests the kind of experience we might be looking for as well as its prospect. It becomes the image of a possibility.

That there is an inner life and an inner world, somehow beyond sense and matter, is not a Greek discovery, nor are we able to speak at all of its first discovery except perhaps by tracing the very emergence of man himself or by listening to the earliest accounts of his origins. For this awareness of spirit and spiritual realities seems to be coeval with man, testified to in his images and, perhaps most dramatically, in his tombs. To draw a bison and to see and appreciate this image is to discover that bisons exist in thought as well as in sense; for the artist had to *have in mind* a bison as he drew it. We may also imagine, since we too know, the shock of feeling something or someone, a moment ago alive, become heavy and limp and lifeless in our hands or arms. Perhaps I may be permitted here an example from my own life's experience. My son, when only three years of age, had a turtle, a gift, of which he was barely fond. When this turtle died, as most turtles do, almost at once and with astonishingly little drama, we brought our son along as we took the turtle to our garden. There was no ritual or pathos. We had in mind for our son no ponderous lesson about death but a simple one about life, namely, that when pets die they are to be buried and not thrown in the trash; a brief unspoken lesson about the respect due to life was the most we had in mind. Instead, as I quickly and unceremoniously covered the turtle with dirt, my son clung to my leg, trembling. I asked him what was the matter, since I knew he couldn't have been feeling grief over a turtle for which he had cared so little. No, he said quite starkly, "I'm frightened. I'm going to die someday." It seems that we are not required to set out on distant digs to discern the origin of our awareness of spirit, its life and its death. It is not a particularly advanced discovery and, as I have said, it is not peculiarly Greek. What is characteristically Greek, however, is to experience and to conceive of the life of spirit as a life of sight and to experience and conceive of the world of spirit as a visible world. "Of sight," writes Philo, "that which is exercised by means of the eyes is the most excellent of all the outward senses, since by that alone all the most beautiful of existing things are comprehended, the sun and the moon, and the whole heaven, and the whole world; but the sight of the soul . . . excels all the other powers of the soul . . . and the soul, feasting on a continuous series of spectacles, has an insatiable desire for beholding such."[8] In saying this, Philo is preserving what is both obvious and essential to the Greek view of mind, spiritual life, and understanding. He is saying what anyone would say who has a mind, who has eyes, to see.

Plato places inner sight and outer sight along a single line and yet there is a great divide between the two. The line is divided into four sections but the most crucial division is the middle one between inner and outer, immaterial and material. While it is true that each of the qualities which we have discerned, and others which might be discerned, within outer or sensory sight serve to describe the Greek understanding of inner or spiritual sight, the two are often contrasted starkly and intransigently. The key to this division, even divorce, lies not with anything peculiar to seeing but, rather, in the irreconcilable qualities of matter and spirit. As I have already suggested, since man does suffer the final necessity, death, the central distinction between what dies and what does not die is transformed into the distinction between what suffers diminishment and what does not suffer diminishment. Finally, since common life is of altogether central concern to the Greeks (and is of appropriately essential concern to all men who must endure together a common, insufferable fate and who find, as well, a beauty and a grandeur that requires to be shared if it is to be enjoyed fully), finally, this distinction is drawn between what suffers diminishment as it is shared and what does not suffer diminishment as it is shared, namely, what is both essentially good and essentially common. This common good which permits, supports, and calls for men's communing in it brings together Greek life and Greek concerns (practical and theoretical, political and religious) to a focus and a fullness whch finds its perhaps most perfect expression in Plato's *Republic*. The *Republic*'s central images are those of the sun, the divided line, and the cave; and all three are visual images for profoundly visual realities. And these images and the entire marathon discussion of the *Republic* arise in response to the threat of Thrasymachus whose claims we have already briefly considered—that each man is at essential odds with each other man as they struggle to the death to collect an uncollectable world, to consume what cannot ever satisfy one's desires and what cannot be shared without deepening one's dissatisfaction.

Here we have the divorce between sense and non-sense, matter and spirit, articulated in political, moral and characteristically Greek terms. For Thrasymachus, the human vocation is quite clearly one of tyranny, because his world is one which denies him his fill; and yet he knows that human life is mostly compromise, because men mostly prefer the secure fruit of placid exploitation to the precarious booty of warring plunder. But, make no mistake, man's most heartfelt dreams are dreams of tyranny and of the absolute power which could alone sustain effective tyranny. This claim of Thrasymachus arises from an experience of matter as primary over spirit and from an experience of both which is closer to touch than to sight. In short, matter is unshareable, drastically so, and spirit is cunning. This image of man, his world, his possibilities is embodied in the impressively ruthless line of Homeric heroes and mythical tyrants singularly epitomized in the sly Odysseus, whom we have seen already; and the true Greek objection to and, I think, devastating rebuttal of this image of man is spoken by Philoctetes when he accuses Odysseus of having a "shabby slit-eyed soul." Shall matter, so clearly unshareable and insufficient, serve as the pattern for man's peculiar possibilities of spirit and thus for craft and tyranny; or shall spirit, so free and sufficient and ineffectual, serve as the precedent for man's physical efforts and ambitions which then become modest and nonviolent? It is precisely this question which Socrates tells Phaedrus is of such urgent and consuming concern to him that he finds it difficult to entertain more remotely speculative questions:

> . . . And I'll tell you why, my friend. I can't as yet "know myself" as the inscription at Delphi enjoins, and so long as that ignorance remains it seems to me ridiculous to inquire into extraneous matters. Consequently I don't bother about such things, but accept the current beliefs about them, and direct my inquiries, as I have

> just said, rather to myself, to discover whether I really am a more complex creature and more puffed up with pride than Typhon, or a simpler, gentler being whom heaven has blessed with a quiet, un-Typhonic nature?[9]

The one single question which draws together and preoccupies Greek thought—scientific, artistic, political, moral, historical, dramatic, and philosophical—is this question of nature (*physis*); specifically human nature. *Physis*, from the word to beget and to grow, describes the full growth and development of a living thing from its embryonic state to its state of full being. A thing's *physis* embraces and accounts for the process of that thing's coming to be what it meant from the very beginning for that thing to be but which is manifest and fully real only when it has in fact come to be that. This final state of completion or perfection or, simply, being, is peculiar to each thing. The possibilities of an acorn and of an infant are from the beginning not the same and their own proper becomings and beings will thus not be the same. This final state of *physis*, the final state of a thing's being, marking not the end of its existence but the end of its becoming, the realization which ends all unrealization, is called *aretē* or excellence. To know the end or term of human *physis*, to know what all human becoming, possibilities, unrealization, desires, and energies reach towards, knowingly or unknowingly, is to know the look (*eidos*) of human *aretē*. When you see a gull soaring easily and gliding with the winds or when you see a goose strutting and hissing arrogantly across a barnyard you know the look of a gull or of a goose, you know what it properly is and does, or quite simply, you know one when you see one. Now, we must recall our earlier discussion of human nature when we saw that human coming-to-be is not a matter of necessity but of freedom, a matter of choice. Except at a circus which is as grotesque an instance of human tyranny over the non-human as one can imagine, one doesn't see elephants walking on two feet or lions dancing, for these activities do not come naturally to them. And yet one might find man doing practically anything (or teaching animals to do practically anything), for most anything comes naturally to a man after a while. Again, quite simply, man is a creature of habit, a creation of his own first choices; for "it is surely inevitable that a man should grow like whatever he enjoys, whether good or bad, even though he may be ashamed to approve it. The result is absolutely inevitable—and what result could we call more momentous for good or evil?"[10] Like shall love like—the good what is good and the evil what is evil—and what a man is like is determined by what he first loves. And what he first loves will be what he first sees as approved and thus as approvable. The eye is quickly blinded by its loves to all else and the inexperienced eye is all but blind from the start to what it has never known. One first loves blindly and one is blinded ever after by the loves one has formed. And thus education (*paideia*), the informing and the guiding of a child's first choices, is the principal work of the *polis*; for so it fashions and characterizes its own life, its own culture.

These three words and the realities which they name describe the core of essentially Greek concerns and ensoul the corpus of Greek literature: nature (*physis*), excellence (*aretē*), and education (*paideia*). Human possibilities and human becoming (*physis*) have a vast spectrum of conceivable outcomes, which means that different men have different ideas of human achievement (*aretē*), and which idea prevails is what is at stake in the nurture (*paideia*) of the young when the most critical life-decisions are made and when one's vision of one's possibilities is thus fixed mostly for life. Finally, education is the proper work not only of the schools but more broadly of the laws and customs (the same word, *nomoi*) of a people; for individual character is largely a product of shared character and collective habit. Although one's hopes for the freedom and the depth of any city's laws, any people's common articulation of human *physis* and *aretē*, must be modest, the setting down of laws is a matter of utter seriousness and of sacred significance. The stakes, the alternatives, for a people are sharply stated by Plato in the *Laws* in words to which we have already attended:

> Now man we call a gentle creature, but in truth, though he is wont to prove more godlike and gentle than any if he have but the right native endowments and the right schooling, let him be trained insufficiently or amiss, and he will show himself more savage than anything on the face of the earth.[11]

It was in the assembly and above all in the theater (which, we recall, means the "seeing-place") that the most public deliberations and debates occurred over the true character, the true look (*eidos*) or form (*morphē*) of human nature and excellence. It was here in the theater that the sharpest, most fatefully consequential alternatives—matter or spirit, tyranny or communion, power or weakness—were articulated to the point of sheer visibility and contrasted with all of the intransigent hostility of darkness and light, blindness and sight. The work of the theater is not entertainment but education (*paideia*), the rearing of a proud people into the full light of day and into the full being of their shared humanity. I say "proud" because every creature takes a certain natural measured pride in its own being what it is and what it was to be; and it is the work of the theater to lay bare, to bring to light and shape and color, the basis not only for Athenian pride but for human pride. Each playwright presents a world, a visible world, a vision of human nature in its becoming, its diminishment, its demise, and its occasional shining fullness. Each plot (*mythos*) verges on and unfolds into the timeless, originating in and driving towards a vision of man as he always properly is and was to be. The Greeks, and surely the Athenians, live mostly with the sea in sight; their landscapes, rugged and finite, are spread out somehow between the sky and the sea which are limitless and always present. They live at water's edge; and they think at eternity's edge. The theater is a place of thought-and-speech (one word and thus one reality in Greek, *logos*) where the world is lucidly gathered together (the first meaning of *legein*, to think-and-speak) just as a people is gathered together to see and to be seen in their original unity—free and available and well-suited and sufficient for one another. In this seeing-place, a people is made to experience the sight of their own nature as see-ers in a precarious balance between darkness and light, blindness and vision, and so to confront their own *paideia*, its choices and their consequences. We may imagine the original viewers of *Philoctetes*, young and old, being drawn from their caves of youthful subservience and mature cynicism, like the young Neoptolemus and the old Philoctetes, and schooled in *philia*, trust and caring, honesty and compassion, or simply in friendship, the only true bond amongst people who must live as one between the same earth and the same sun, enduring the same fate.

Then too we may appropriately recall the young Oedipus, acclaimed, effectual, and self-assured. The sphinx terrorizes the people of Thebes and bargains with them for a solution to his riddle—who makes his way first on four feet, next on two, and finally on three? And Oedipus responds simply—man. By solving this insubstantial, playful riddle, Oedipus frees the Thebans from a cursed fate which could only be lifted by dispelling their ignorance which proved to be an ignorance of "man." And it is Oedipus' glib and insubstantial understanding of "man," his unaccountable knack for saying the right thing at the right time, quite unknowingly, a knack which soon fails him, that wins for him the confidence of a people and entitles him to rule over them. In due course, his profound ignorance brings a curse upon this people and he dismisses the only man of vision, blind old Teiresias, with arrogant and unwarranted disrespect.

Oedipus first appears to be the very figure of competence and self-assurance and yet he is undone swiftly and thoroughly by his own astounding blindness. What all who have eyes to see, including Oedipus himself, come soon to see is that Oedipus does not know what he did and is doing (i.e., that he murdered his father and married his mother) and has essentially violated his own nature because he did not know himself. In what seems at first an act of despair and desperate retribution, Oedipus plunges himself into darkness, gouging his eyes until they stream down gore over his barely discernible face. In fact, this stream of blood is the afterbirth of his own renewal and second birth. He enters his mother's womb again not only in incest but in an unheard of conversion, the character of which is not clear until many long years later, in the lives of both Oedipus and Sophocles. For now Oedipus falls to his palms and knees and makes his way four-footed, as a beast or as an infant. The riddle begins afresh; and this time its truth shall be lived and grasped with the suffering and patience which alone brings true wisdom. Years later, the aged Sophocles will bring back the aged Oedipus, in *Oedipus at Colonus*, tapping his way with a seeming helplessness as Teiresias once had, himself confronting an arrogant, spiritually witless, sightless young king, as he had once been. This time, in his wisdom, his clear-sightedness, he claims only what is just and his to claim, a resting place, and to bring not a curse but a blessing. He comes as a simpler, gentler being whom heaven has blessed with a quiet, un-Typhonic nature.

Like Colonus to one side of the stage, Oedipus himself becomes a legend, transfigured and eternal. He leaves behind him no trace but only a bewildering mystery; and those who remain, their eyes blinded with tears, are left only to guess what has become of Oedipus and what shall become of us. Perhaps annihilation, perhaps the mere setting of one sun which will yield to the rising of another and to the disclosure of another world to be known. It seems there is no knowing this, at least not without still another birth, still another turning, whose time has come for Oedipus but not yet for us. We are told instead only to "let the weeping cease; / Let no one mourn again / These things are in the hands of God."[12] As for the years between Oedipus' departure from Thebes and his entrance into Athens, the years between *Oedipus the King* and *Oedipus at Colonus*, the years of *paideia* for both Oedipus and Sophocles, years of patient suffering and the recovering of sight, we are told only to

> Think of some shore in the north the
> Concussive waves make stream
> This way and that in the gales of winter:
> It is like that with him:
> The wild wrack breaking over him
> From head to foot, and coming on for ever;
> Now from the plunging down of the sun,
> Now from the sunrise quarter,
> Now from where the noonday gleams,
> Now from the night and the north.[13]

As eyes, long accustomed to darkness, first confront the light, they are more thoroughly blinded than they have ever been. Thus it was with the inhabitants of Plato's cave and so it was with Oedipus. The first glimpse of the light of day, of the full light of being, is overwhelming, suddenly, and all at once. One can make out nothing in particular. One seems to be staring into the sun itself, straight on, whereas in fact it is the most distant, deflected rays which have found their way to squinting cast-aside eyes. This first state of sight is a foretaste, however, of what it will one day be like to stare into the sun itself, straight on. Between these two blindingly full-sighted moments lies a world of quite particular sights to be seen, one at a time, time and again. So too, wonder, the beginning of wisdom, a wordless, almost witless, amazement at the sheer presence of being rather than nonbeing, is as incompetent and futile a posture as any thinker might assume. And yet it too is a glimpse and a foretaste of the moment of pure beholding towards which all true thinking works its way back and forth. Between these two moments of sight, the first and the last, when one is simply blinded to all else by a light overpowering in its presence, a pure gift not to be denied, there is no avoiding the ambiguity of darkness and light, blindness and sight, so susceptible to illusion and to habit are men's eyes and their souls, their capacities for the light and for the truth. Each man will inevitably live as far as he can see and see only as far as he lives; some will live with a muscular and moral squint, others will meet their lives straight on and clear-sightedly. And yet what is seen is seen and is there; and sight will always be the proper judge of blindness, although blindness will continue to presume to judge the sight of others. One may only hope for the mutual convergence of power and wisdom, sovereignty and vision; or for a two-eyed, clear-sighted god who will finally resolve the irreconcilable differences of partially sighted, partially blind, men, quarreling in their caves over shadows and secondhand truths.

Whatever the formal context—whether the assembly or the academy or the theater or wherever—the Greek mind is centered on and preoccupied with the question of human nature and excellence, the rearing of the one and the attainment of the other. And the object of this inquiry is characteristically imagined to be an object of sight, something to be seen which is present always and ever accessible, to be known in its many appearances, freely studied at one's own initiative and leisure, withholding itself from no one and altering itself for no one, requiring only the perfection of one's openness and honesty and oneness of vision and of heart to be disclosed and grasped. What is quite interesting and significant, and yet what lies beyond the scope of these reflections to explore in any detail, is that it was in medical speculation and practice that human *physis*, human nature, first became the controlling center of a formal study and of a sustained literary effort. This original link between medicine and *physis* is retained in our term, physician, for medical doctor. The formal object, then, of Greek medical inquiry is human *physis*, the nature of man as a peculiar form of life, a peculiar organism. This inquiry into human nature is not to be separate, in Greek speculation, from inquiry into the great nature, the Nature of the Universe, of the whole (*phusis tou pantos*). In fact, it is this earlier Ionian conception of Nature, which Greek medical theorists extend to the study of man's physical nature and which guides, as well, later philosophical understandings of man's spiritual nature. And in all of these inquiries and understandings there is an essential, if not ever fully realized, unity; for Greek culture is always the culture of the body as well as of the soul and of both in relation to the larger whole and the fuller unity in which they participate.

Central to all of these reflections are, then, the ideas of mixture and harmony, fundamental for and common to Greek medicine and natural philosophy. Harmony in medicine, of course, means health which is not precisely the same for all. What is suitable for the sustenance or the recovery of one man's health may be quite injurious to another's. It is always a matter of feeling or judgment (*aisthēsis*, the word for visual perception), says the unknown author of *On Ancient Medicine*, a voice of the school of Hippocrates. In this same text the doctor and the pilot are likened to each other, a comparison which Plato and Aristotle later use to describe what it means to *aim* at what never changes in the midst of what is ever changing, namely, to describe practical or ethical or aesthetic or political wisdom, which is a kind of sight but also a kind of feeling or cunning or skill. To aim suggests this mixture or middle ground between the mark and the aiming, between what is properly an object of pure sight and what involves a range of timeful activities and concerns and senses. Greek ethics, art, politics, and medicine are dominated by the conception of suitability or appropriateness which always implies some initial, neither fully knowing nor simply unknowing, glimpse of that to which some diet or law or habit or curve is suitable or appropriate. To practical sight, a kind of half-sight, distracted and diverted and immersed in the nonvisual, this *to which* is never disclosed and yet never wholly concealed.

There is, then, no question of a simply timeless standard of health and illness, or of immutable states of one's body, to be seen once and for all, and ever after applied with an all-knowing exactitude. Neither is human nature each time unique admitting of no general, shareable experience or understanding. The object of Greek medicine, the "truth" of man's organism, namely, man's physical nature, belongs at the same time both to the realm of the visible, somehow common and timeless, and to the realm of the invisible, always particular and timeful. Thus the Greeks rightfully distinguish the layman from the physician. The layman sees each symptom for the first time wholly divorced from any sense of human nature or of Nature itself. He doesn't know if he is to be alarmed at a particular blemish or discomfort or dysfunction, nor does he know how to treat such problems. Without any precedents in his experience, he doesn't know whether a particular painful limb or organ ought to be soaked or amputated or rubbed or ignored. Nothing looks like anything else and thus symptoms are meaningless for they symptomize nothing. Such a man, the layman, the Greeks call *idiotēs* (whence our "idiot"), one who lives in his own world, blind to and inexperienced in all else.

The doctor, on the other hand, is a *demiourgos*, a public worker, one whose vision encompasses the form of things beyond the shape of his own private life. To see one child born, one plague victim, one fever's course is not to have seen them all, at once; and yet it will mean that when one sees another such occurrence or victim one will truly be able to say that he is not seeing it for the first time. The eye, the aim, the feel of the physician is slowly schooled and skilled to discern the natural and the naturally suitable without giving way to rash general hypotheses which cannot but lead to disastrous particular consequences. The medical *demiourgos,* like the Platonic *demiourgos,* is one who knows and acts in harmony with the look of things, the look of the whole, namely, in harmony with each nature and with Nature itself.

It is this understanding of sighted action, responsible and true to the mark, which serves as a model for each area of Greek life. Solon, the sixth-century poet and political reformer, develops an organic theory of the state, its health and its diseases, its calms and its storms, and the laws of each. Tyranny is seen to follow as surely from the collection of power in the hands of a few men as does hail and snow fall from the menace of dark, brooding clouds. And Thucydides says that he writes a history not for his own generation but a history which will last forever; for history repeats itself to the discerning eye just as to the same eye man never essentially changes. Thus Thucydides provides us with a calculus of power, its uses and abuses, and a study of the character of tyranny and empire which is confirmed by *The Prince, Mein Kampf,* and daily experience. He is convinced that the great war between Athens and Sparta will be seen again as will the plague; and so he is minutely careful to describe the symptoms and stages of both to assure their future recognition.

Likewise, the sophists, for their part, claim that an understanding of human nature (*physis*) is the only truly adequate foundation for education, which was their central concern. From the sophist tradition there emerges Socrates who claims that medicine provides the exemplary pattern for true rhetoric, namely, his own art of political philosophy. Plato models his own classification of plants and animals, and his entire dialectic system of classification, upon that of Hippocrates. And finally, Plato and Aristotle speak of the soul's well-being (*eudaimonia*), the fullness of human being, as health, likening the excellences (*aretai*) of the soul to those of the body. One is born into the life of philosophy and no one is first or finally responsible for his own soul's being. One's very life is begotten, eased into its first moments' light by a midwife and reared to full stature and sight, to full health and harmony with the whole of one's nature and with the whole of Nature itself. For this entire movement or course of coming-to-be there is but one central pervasive image—that of sight—which has guided our brief excursion through Greek drama, medicine, politics, and history and which we have yet to follow to its perfection, a perfection perhaps most clearly and extremely formulated by Aristotle.

For Aristotle it is the experience of wonder, the experience of being shocked and held still by the spectacle of being, which begins the life of inner inquiry and sight and which provides that life with sufficient warrant and direction. Each insight will bring with it its own assurance, the assurance of what is seen, and yet nothing so unquestionably real as this first experience until the moment of contemplation of which it is a first bestowal. Wonder is both playful and needful, begotten as man is from fullness and poverty, a glimpse of the essentially overflowing and exceedingly restless character of most of human life. The sun is the most common and appropriate image of this overflow towards which man is drawn, paradoxically, in freedom, leisure, and utter need, as to the source of his being and to the completion of his nature. Human *paideia*, the rearing of man as one who is born to see, is complete, and human nature is perfect, only in the activity of contemplation, the pure beholding of the divine. The *eidos*, the idea of man, is dark and formless, like a closed eye or an eye without light, until it is opened to and filled with the forms and light of other beings and finally of being itself. There is nothing less private than man, or the eye, neither of which have any reality to themselves, apart and distinct from those objects for which they have the capacity. The being of man is indeed like that of the eye, capacious for all that the light discloses to it and finally for the light's own disclosure of itself. The proper work (*ergon*) of man is to gather, to collect, (*legein*), to think and speak the world together in its original and timeless unity by glimpsing the wholeness and oneness of all things in the divine mind. The human mind (*nous*), the highest and fullest and purest thing in man, is a sharing in, a communing in, the divine mind and thus in the divinity of all things. And the being-at-work of man (*energeia*) is a restless, excessive, sharing in the being-at-work, the coming-to-be of all things as they find themselves one and whole in man's vision of them, as they have always been. Man is formless matter, material to be worked upon, to be made real and actual by the being-at-work of all things and so to become all things. The eye is somehow all that it sees and man is somehow all that he knows. The world is one and whole and requires for its perfection only to be known by man—for the most part studiously, discursively, inquiringly, even hypothetically; and yet, in rare gifted moments, all at once, unsparingly and wondrously.

If man lives in accord with mind (*nous*), in accord with the highest thing in him, he is nothing except what fullness of the world he comes to know. Man has no peculiar possibilities of his own except to guess the riddles of the eternal and to suffer the pain and the delight of their truth. Human mind, man in the fullest sense and spirit, "is invisible, though it sees everything itself; and it has an essence which is undiscernible, though it can discern the essences of all other things."[14] Man understands himself when he comes to understand the universe of things; the possibilities of the one image, the possibilities of the other. To give an account of human nature is to give an account of Nature in its essential humanity and divinity. There are no finally appropriate limits to human wakefulness and sight, neither those of the body nor those of the city. The life of the see-er is one of sheer wakefulness to all that discloses itself, from the most distant star to the most common wildflower. Thus Aristotle had Alexander bring back every manner of new sight from his conquests and Diogenes Laertius tells of Aristotle that he slept with a steel ball in his hand stretched out over a metal pan. When he dropped off he also let the ball fall from his hand; and the clatter woke him, renewed, and able to return to his wakefulness and reflection and sight. We are left only to imagine the passion and intensity and fullness of a life so jealous of itself and so dreading of the slightest interruption. And yet man's life of wakefulness is fated to frequent and final interruption. Man, insofar as he is wakeful and thus sightful, is godlike but he cannot elude the concerns of body and city altogether or finally. Erect, standing between the earth and sky, man's true posture leaves his eyes free to range across the whole; and the natural horizon of his becoming is the cosmos, the loveliness and order of the whole. And yet piety and obedience, weariness, passion, and finally death cause him to bow down now and again and forever.

> . . . He shares the godlike manner of being. . . . But this sharing is an intermittent one; ever so often overcome by fatigue, his wakefullness yields to sleep. He has to lie down. His divinity is but a passing shadow—as is his very life.[15]

Such a life is necessarily forgetful of its own individual tragedy, the extent of its suffering, the brevity of its joys, and the depth of its imperfections. Such a life cannot finally care deeply for itself, a life lived briefly only once. Man the see-er is not allowed to take himself in his unique particularity at all seriously. He is nothing but what he sees in the presence of his seeing it; and his sight is always either partial or intermittent, and mostly both. Man glimpses being, reflects briefly the image, the glow, of being in his eyes and soul, and then becomes opaque, impervious—a dull spiritless stone among stones. In point of fact, man never escapes the cave; he becomes not divine but a plaything of the divine, with no peculiar or legitimate claims of his own. He is but a "short-lived heaven" says Philo, a passing shadow; these words return us to the parable of the cave and to a more severe and, I think, a reading more faithful to the aging Plato. Perhaps there is no true ascent from the cave; perhaps men may aspire to be no more than the puppets in the hands of the captors who may themselves be the gods. "Let us look at the whole matter," says Plato in the *Laws*, "in some such light as this. We imagine that each of us living creatures is a puppet made by the gods, possibly as a plaything, or possibly with some more serious purpose."[16]

Time is the "changing image of the eternal," says Plato; and man finally belongs to time. Each man is held up briefly to the light, to collect, to reflect, to mirror, to embody, to shadow that light for a moment. The truest life, the eminently shining and truthful life of Plato's guardian, who is to be "the spector of all time and of all existence," is filled to overflowing and then emptied, utterly despoiled, to all appearances abandoned by its gods, breathless and unvisited. Man's eyes and soul are, it seems, finally dark and unknowing in the hands of the dark and inaccessible divine purpose. There is something playful about sight, something illusorily free and naïve and irresponsible, and thus something not finally serious.

> Why, I mean, we should keep our seriousness for serious things, and not waste it on trifles, and that, while God is the real goal of beneficent serious endeavor, man, so we said before, has been constructed as a toy for God, and this is, in fact, the finest thing about him.[17]

Man is not finally sightful but blind. His world is finally eclipsed by the sheer distance and otherness of the divine source which draws him beyond his own humanity without then disclosing its own divinity. Man, left without discernible limits and coherent purpose, is left to regard himself playfully, drawn up into a game, a laughter, a joy in which he takes part unknowingly, obediently, trustfully. So we will think it strange, says Aristotle, that his vision of man leads him beyond anything intelligently, discernibly human; but he has no true choice but to live in accord with his highest possibilities, even if this pursuit leaves man a stranger to himself lost in complicity with a strange God who does not let himself be seen. But we are told we mustn't weep in the face of bewildering mystery, for tears cloud the eyes and bemuse the spirit, that we mustn't take it all too seriously; for "these things are in the hands of God." They stand fast and possess unquestionable validity, as does the life of man in their grip.

NOTES

1. Henri Bergson, *The Creative Mind*, trans. Mabelle L. Andison (New York: Greenwood Press, 1968), pp. 161, 163.

2. Karl Jaspers, *Three Essays: Leonardo, Descartes, Max Weber*, trans. Ralph Manheim (New York: Harcourt, Brace & World, 1964), pp. 25–26.

3. See Cicero *Tusculan Disputations* 5. 3. 8–9; 5. 12. 58–59.

4. Iamblichus *De vita Pythagorica* 12. 58–59, Codex Florentinus, recen. Augustus Nauck (Petropoli, 1884), pp. 39–41.

5. In discussing the ideas of Leonardo, I will be referring to his formulation of those ideas in his *Treatise on Painting*, Codex Urbinas Latinus 1270, trans. A. Philip McMahor (Princeton: Princeton University Press, 1956).

6. Arthur Schopenhauer, *The World as Will and Representation* (New York: Dover Publications, 1966), 2:28.

7. Hans Jonas, *The Phenomenon of Life* (New York: Dell, 1966), p. 148.

8. Nahum Glatzer, ed., *The Essential Philo* (New York: Schocken, 1971), pp. 94, 15.

9. Plato *Phaedrus* 230a, trans. R. Hackforth in *Plato: The Collected Dialogues*, ed. Edith Hamilton and Huntington Cairns, Bollingen Series, No. 71 (New York: Pantheon Books, 1961).

10. Plato *Laws* 2. 6566, trans. A. E. Taylor, in *Collected Dialogues*.

11. Ibid., 6. 766a.

12. Sophocles *Oedipus at Colonus*, trans. Robert Fitzgerald (Chicago: University of Chicago Press, 1954), ll. 1777–79, the last lines of the play. A more literal translation of the last, most enigmatic line is offered by Jebb: "verily these things stand fast."

13. Ibid., ll. 1238–48.

14. Glatzer, p. 20.

15. From the transcript of a lecture delivered by Professor Jacob Klein at the University of Chicago, January 11, 1966.

16. Plato *Laws* 677d.

17. Ibid., 803c.

Even if you do not see you shall see by hearing. . . . He who will not take hold with his ears but wants to look with his eyes is lost. . . . Stick your eyes in your ears.

Martin Luther

CHAPTER FIVE

HEARING

The sightful gaze of the contemplative which brings such fullness and completion to the soul of man the see-er requires a sure distance from the dark, the demonic, and the damned which is simply not available to most men and not acceptable to many others. The peculiar tranquillity, the leisured, still, disengagement which seeing both assumes and bestows is often, perhaps always, not at all a matter of being privileged to live in a time free of exigence and evil. Rather, it seems to be a matter of turning away from and of being held still within the swiftest, most urgent, most disquieting necessities. This frightful frenzy of unavoidable and uncontrollable events may be seen to haunt the dialogues of Plato without ever fully intruding or interrupting those conversations held in the darkest of times. Thus we find the *Theaetetus*, one of the most speculative of the dialogues, framed by the imminent death of young Theaetetus at the outset and by the imminent death of Socrates at its conclusion. Somehow, in the face of the needless death of the city's most promising youth and in prospect of the groundless condemnation of the city's most estimable citizen, there is time for stillness and remove and wholehearted consideration of what has no direct bearing on, no saving power over, those tragic times and places and those lives lived there only once, briefly. Rather, it must be a matter of the unquestioned primacy, the all-consuming presence, of what is beyond time and change, beyond what must be done or suffered now or never again, beyond what is lived now never to be relived. And yet it is not only the timeless which we find so consuming and compelling. Achilles and Priam, their hearts crushed beneath a grief unshareable and hardly to be borne—and yet both shared and endured together—their eyes washed and glistening with tears and for those never to return, *wonder*, Homer tells us, at each other.

There is indeed a wonder proper to the altogether ephemeral yet altogether splendorous deeds, forgiven failings, risings or fallings, of fated men and women. There are stories—often grim and uncomely and savage—which nevertheless fit and suit our sense of things and which must be told, just as there are lives—often equally wretched and hapless—which seemingly had to have been lived. And in the telling and in the listening we find these stories truthful; just as in the living of our lives we find a truth which comes only with laughter or tears, a truth which comes only with a knowing, accepting immersion into the stream of our lives' moments—whether deadeningly slow or ravagingly furious or measured and mediocre. There are moments which, like bits of spray in an endless sea, exist apart in the sun's day for a mere instant and then are lost again forever, moments which nevertheless seem to shine more alluringly than the sun itself for men who know themselves to be cast up and out like a fine mist against a blazing sky rather than situated calm and eternal like a moon reflecting the sun painlessly forever. Sophocles has surely grasped the passionate and tragic individuality of life lived always only once, fated to be misunderstood, spoiled, destroyed, and lost, in this decidedly Dionysian image spoken by Deianeira in *The Women of Trachis*:

> I see something
> unspeakable, incomprehensible to human reason.
> Somehow I had happened to throw the ball of wool,
> which I had used to smear the robe, into the full heat
> of the sun's rays, and, as it became warm,
> it all ran together, a confused mass, and crumbled
> to bits on the ground, looking most like the dust
> one sees eaten away in the cutting of a piece of wood.
> Like this it lies where it fell. But from the earth
> on which it rests, clotted foam boils up
> like the rich liquid of the blue-green fruit
> from the vines of Dionysius, poured on the earth
> And now I do not know what to think. . . .[1]

There is a beauty to what passes and must pass which is enhanced by its passing. We are mortals and we have a privileged appreciation for the loveliness, the rage, the trembling urgency of what perishes and what knows that it is being consumed even as it shines. This peculiar beauty is held captive in these few brief lines, delicate and powerful, at which we must wonder:

> Think of Leonidas perhaps and the hoplites
> glittering with liberation,
> as they combed one another's golden Botticellian
> hair at Thermopylae—friends and lovers,
> the bride and the bridegroom—
> and moved into position to die.[2]

And, regardless of this beauty proper to the fleeting lives of fated individuals, the primacy of the timeless is questioned by those moments, so shadowed, so apace, so encircling and constraining, that stillness and distance become the prerogatives of the dreaming and of the deranged; and such moments seem to prevail among men and women living under the curse of Cain for whom the earth and their own bodies bear fruit—always sparingly, always perishingly—only at the heavy cost of consuming toil and pain. There is an inescapable primacy to the everyday, to the toilsome trouble and pain of existence; and there is a corresponding primacy to whatever brings solace in the midst of, or even salvation from, a doom too close, too relentlessly on the move to allow for the festival of poetic vision with which the *Iliad* ends (and with which it began and unfolds), much less the celebration of the contemplative at the splendor of being. Our fate is a violent fate and our salvation must be so violent as to overwhelm it and carry us away. There is a darkness at the center of our sight, a deep trust uttered in a silence which, if it remains silent forever, must radically question that trust. The presence, the eternity, the reality of light, is finally an assumption, a blind faith; and regarding our own origins, the origins of our world, and their end, we are left with only likely tales, we are left in the hands of the gods whose distance and whose silence, if never bridged, never broken, brings terror and doubt and darkness.

If we close our eyes or enter sheer darkness, we notice at once that our attention to silence and sound is keenly sharpened and heightened. It first seems as if sounds are "next in line" for our concern, a fourth, more obscure and faint, dimension of sight. That is, we may at first continue to think of ourselves as see-ers, now forced to see with our ears, grasping the audible shadows of things once seen and whose forms must now be imagined at the suggestion of visibly meaningful sounds. However, as our sightlessness persists and as sufficient time passes for us to question whether we any longer know the look of those sounds around us, namely, as we encounter visually unfamiliar sounds, we slowly become hearers and no longer, or at least no longer primarily, see-ers—our bias for sight and sights is weakened and what we encounter is strange, insecurely ours, other, and quite possibly threatening. Again Schopenhauer interestingly comments that deaf-mutes, once cured of their deafness by galvanism, become deadly pale with terror at their first encounters with sound. We are sighted and mobile beings and there is a decisive correlation between our capacity for sight and our capacity for swift, directed motion. We are able to see from afar the objects of our desires and of our fears, and to pursue or to flee each in time. We are upright and swift of foot, our hands free to seize or to ward off. What this means is that imaginatively and emotionally we are predators and are ourselves prey; we are accustomed and required to sight the objects of longing and dread from afar. When our eyes are darkened, we are left with long-ranging desires and fears and energies but without the capacity to identify and distinguish the desirous from the dreadful, and thus to direct ourselves towards the one and away from the other. We glimpse our most primitive premises as animals of prey when we find ourselves in sudden and unyielding darkness and we glimpse our queer boundarylessness as soulful humans when we fall into the deepest confusions and doubts. So long as our blindness encounters only silence, we cannot but be preoccupied with the absence of sight; but when that blind silence is broken, we are no longer see-ers but hearers, neither predators nor prey, but the playthings of the gods in a world of only likely tales, not even told for us. And it is this world of sounds and music and stories and hearing and shouting and believing that we will now briefly explore.

For the moment, suppose that we are utterly in the dark, sealed into a thick silence. Then a single note is struck. We start at its sound and linger with its resonance. Again there is silence and we realize that we are now listening only to the echo of the sound in our memory and no longer to the trailing reverberations of the sound itself. Finally the memory fades and we are left to anticipate another sound. The ear, and we as hearers, must await the event of sound each time anew. The silence from which sounds emerge is more impenetrable, more unpredictable than the darkest darkness of night or shadow. There are no days and nights in the world of the ear, no regular pattern of sound and silence, which would permit the ear its leisure and rest. Rather, the ear is never closed but always attentive and on call to the eruptive eventfulness of sound, the pure creature of change and movement and time. In short, there is no light of day for the ear; its world is never copresent with it, available, disclosed, all at once. Rather, its realities are born of silence which is utterly impervious to the ear. Sounds unfold across time and belong to time, to now and not then, to then and not now; and the ear too must be given over to those same times, must be contemporaneous with its sounds, for it to hear them at all.

It takes time for any sound to occur and to be heard, just as any form, any sight, requires space to be visible and to be seen. Sounds are necessarily extended in time even as sights are extended in space. The ear, if it is to serve us at all, must belong to our full time, open and trustful before it is prejudiced and selective. But it is from the beginning more alert to what is turned towards it, to sounds directed its way, to sounds nearer and louder, to what suggests immediate promise or peril. The thinking ear, the disciplined ear, may accommodate one's preferences in some measure; but the ear remains vulnerable, the victim of sound—our organ for the eventful, the immediate, the exigent, and the personal. Sounds are always directional, meant for some ears and not for others, the privilege of those who happen to be here and not there, now and not then. Each vision of our world or of man presents us with an expanse which takes time to explore and to live fully and there is never enough time. And each time our eyes open we begin all over. Vision seems to squander time and to ignore its passing. The ear listens to the myriad voices of life and death as they articulate and punctuate a timeless visual statement never seen, only glimpsed, to no avail.

We are largely at the mercy of sound for its comings and its passings and for our own life of hearing. One might say that we, as hearers, are the playthings of sound. Each sound calls forth the ear into one or other brief existence, passing it on, tossing it about, and setting it down again where it must wait, remember, and groundlessly imagine its next enlivening. The ear knows well the sudden fright of the unexpected, the attentive faithfulness of the listener, the memory and the hope in which an empty present must dwell and find its fullness. Sound—the eventful, the immediate, the once-for-all, the inescapable—importunes, prys us loose from less urgent concerns, carries us off from our preoccupations and predilections. To live a life of pure hearing is to live the vagary, pointless life of an undiscerning victim, a prey and a pawn, uncritical and unappreciative of whatever comes along. It is to have no life, no mind, no will of one's own. "Accordingly," says Schopenhauer, "the thinking mind lives in eternal peace with the eye, and at eternal war with the ear."[3] So bemusing and distracting and enslaving are sounds, so inherently servile is the ear, that one who lives a life of hearing by living immersed in sound is no longer enabled to live and to think with freedom and leisure. I might suggest that the telephone gives us all a layman's taste of such a state. Schopenhauer offers us some rather curious and rather more extreme comments on such a state of affairs and soul:

> Actually I have for a long time been of the opinion that the quantity of noise anyone can comfortably endure is in inverse proportion to his mental powers, and may therefore be regarded as a rough estimate of them. Therefore, when I hear dogs barking unchecked for hours in the courtyard of a house, I know what to think of the mental powers of the inhabitants. The man who habitually slams doors instead of shutting them with the hand, or allows this to be done in his house, is not merely ill-mannered, but also coarse and narrow-minded.[4]

All sound is merely noise prior to the selection of wanted, pleasant or significant, sounds and to the screening out of the unwanted. Such discriminations are, however, mostly willful and personal. The ear alone knows or registers sound, which is neither noise nor music apart from one's wishes. In fact, it is curious how even the most offensive sounds, if listened to with attentive interest, cease being noise. Noise, then, is unwanted sound; and music is wanted sound or, most properly, music is sound quite literally willed into existence, the creation of man, or of God. The thinking ear fashions and appreciates beautiful sounds in time even as the thinking eye fashions and appreciates beautiful sights in space. However, visual art (at least as this was classically understood) is quite another thing from aural art. The classical painter or sculptor, while not simply copying the visual world, surely takes his bearings from the forms he has come to know as a see-er. Like the Platonic demiurge, the visual artist does not create purely, from the nothingness or the formlessness of a void; rather, he looks to the shapes, the looks of things, with which he fills his eyes and his canvas. Not so with the composer. There is no stable world of sound to which he might refer. He does not surround himself with sounds as he composes, as a painter may paint from a model. Rather, he places himself within silence and reaches more simply, more purely, within himself for the sounds with which to break that silence open and to fill it with voice. Surely there is memory, the sound of a sea or a clock heard and unforgotten; but memory, as Augustine has explored it for us with such imagination and insight, is indeed "a great deep" which wraps the human and the divine into a deep complicity of creation and renewal. For now we may well return to simpler thoughts, however, and claim only that the human ear, man as hearer, is both the creature and the creator of sound and is invariably concerned with the coherence, the harmony, the oneness and significance and beauty of the world. Still more simply, all tin and wooden ears notwithstanding, man the hearer is musical.

Music is the soundful articulation of time. Apart from sound and time, music is plainly inconceivable. Beyond this indisputable claim, it is commonplace for the Greeks and for us to think of time in visual categories, to imagine time as unfolding in perfectly (or near perfectly) even circular motion, visually embodied in the circuit of the sun. There is a truth to the vision of time which permits us watches and calendars and appointments made and kept. In one sense we are all "on the same time" so long as we occupy the same visual space or perspective. And yet it is clear that we are not all on the same time. The time of the old and the time of the young do not proceed apace. A woman has periods of time of which men know very little. It is marvelous when our times coincide, when we are in stride; but lovers, and teachers, and parents, and friends—anyone but the lifelong recluse—know how rare and gracious are such moments when my time is yours and your time mine. This is to say that there is an experience of time, its movement and its measure, which is quite apart from the commonly accessible and shareable world of seeing. Each of us divides our own time into sounds and silence whose duration and pleasure and pain we find it quite difficult to share and to know we have shared.

It is likely that music began with the mere beating of a rhythm, perhaps with sticks or dried bones. Rhythm is simply the division of time into audible intervals. For instance, the same six seconds of clock time might be divided or punctuated by six or twelve or two beats. The extent or duration of the "whole" is the same in each instance, namely, six seconds. However, the various possible rhythms with which we might articulate that whole vary our experience of it. A rapid articulation of time, particularly if we are already on edge or harried, will seem to step up the flow of time, whereas a slow, steady beat will seem to slow it down. The experience, then, of six seconds broken into twelve intervals will not be at all equivalent to the experience of the same six seconds broken into three intervals. Quite simply, they are not the same six seconds, not the same time at all. And if we decide to introduce emphasis into our rhythms, we may add that the experience of six even intervals with emphasis on the odd-numbered beats (ONE-two-THREE-four-FIVE-six) is not at all the same as the experience of the same intervals with the even-numbered beats emphasized (one-TWO-three-FOUR-five-SIX). And, of course, our point is made with increasing cogency as the full range of rhythmic possibilities are considered and explored. The relentlessly steady, driving cadences of marching drums and boots occasions a condition of sense and soul worlds apart from the ecstatically whirling frenzy of fingers and feet that dance away the hours. In each case the matter is simple; it is simply a matter of breaking silence with sounds which we create and "space" in time. This experience of the simplest of musical forms is the experience of pure movement, pure action in time, the experience of time itself and of our own inherent temporality. Sound exists in time and nowhere else and when we create sounds and live in the sounds which we create, we too belong to time and feel the possibilities and the limits, the sheer delight and precariousness of what is so eminently perishable that it begins to die the moment it begins to live. In sound and music we breathe in our mortality and let it out again, knowingly, accepting of the dead silence that encircles and consumes every beat, every note, every voice which ever finds life.

All music, while it divides duration into intervals, strives to put time together again into a shapely whole. And this shaping is possible only through the power of imagination to think the past and to think the future at once. The experience of duration, of extended time, requires that we somehow encompass the unfolding of temporal succession, remembering those moments already experienced as immediately present and anticipating those moments not yet experienced as immediately present. Without a present expanded imaginatively to include the enduring presence of things past and the impinging presence of things future, there could be no experience of temporality—we would exist in time without any self-conscious appreciation of our existence in time or of time's existence in us. Without the reach of memory and expectation we would have no capacity for music or for creation of any sort in time. We would never know a silence or void, the soundful shattering of that void, and the pleasure of our voice as an enduring drama, true of men and of gods; we would never know the "truth" of creation and of time which we may call "coherence." "All music," says Igor Stravinsky, "is nothing more than a succession of impulses that converge toward a definite point of repose."[5]

Music is not merely a matter of passing time but, as we have said, of organizing time into an *organum*, a living whole. Music must not simply start and stop but begin and end and cohere. The truth and goodness and beauty of music is a matter of resolution and coherence which are exceptionally difficult criteria to grasp and give some account of without incessant appeal to soundful instances of each.

If we listen with the least care and appreciation to the rise and the fall of the melodic line in plainsong we have a simple and striking example of musical coherence and resolution. The coiling melody of any piece of Gregorian chant is both supple and taut with a living tension and integrity like the body of a serpent until it is resolved and perishes with the final cadence. Every note is either rising towards or falling away from every other, each tone is preparing for or is prepared for by the others. The more complicated the musical structure, the more elaborate is the organism which must provide life and breath and movement even to its furthest extremities. It is the melody or theme, in all of its simplicity and power of conception, however varied and developed it may become, which brings coherence and resolution—may we say musical "truth"—to a composition. The melody must be brief and telling, presented often and clearly enough to assure recognition and recollection. Its "truth" is inward, a matter of integrity, completion and inevitability, a truthfulness to itself. We are left with saying that it begins and ends and proceeds "as it should." A melodic theme either creates for itself its own compelling criterion and warrant or it fails to commend itself, fails to convince others because it has failed to create a vitality and a centripetal force which draws us into it. We know as we pick up a creature whether it is alive in our hands and we feel its life leave it as it dies. And so we feel the living tension of some music well up in our ears and souls, we live with its movements and perish with it as it draws to its conclusion.

This criterion of organic life and power and movement we bring to music, and other criteria, moral or logical, have no place. A piece of music may be as dissonant in its harmony and irregular in its rhythm and ragged in its melodic line as it likes, so long as we are finally convinced that all was as *it* should have been. Any pure creation must answer only to itself and we may only say whether or not it pleased us or attempt the more demanding judgment whether or not this creation is self-answerable, pure and sincere, whether it "rings true." Truisms whose truth trails away from us. Finally God knows what we mean by such words.

The intrinsic temporality of music is more complicated, however, than we have yet let on: for music is not only created but remembered, perhaps written down, and performed many times over from memory or from the written score. Each time a piece of music is played it is born again to a somehow new life and each time it yields once more to silence it dies another death. And each time we listen to a piece of music we rise and die again with it; for our music like ourselves is mortal and dies in the end, always awaiting rebirth. The creator of a piece of music, then, has a partner across time in each one who will ever presume to perform that music, to bring it to life again. The creature outlives and outreaches his creator, comes to life at others' summons—such is the risk of those creatures who themselves presume to create in time—such, in image, is man (and his god):

> Thus in contrast to the craftsman of the plastic arts, whose finished work is presented to the public eye in an always identical form, the composer runs a perilous risk every time his music is played, as the competent presentation of his work each time depends on the unforeseeable and imponderable factors that go to make up the virtues of fidelity and sympathy, without which the work will be unrecognizable on one occasion, inert in another, and in any case, betrayed.[6]

Fidelity and sympathy—these are the demands placed by any creator upon those who would experience or renew the life of the creation, namely, those who would participate with him in an enduring act of creation. The performer is closer to the creative source than are the mere listeners and thus these demands are heaviest upon him; for "the first impression, which is so important, the first contact of the newborn work, is completely dependent upon the validity of a presentation that eludes all controls."[7] The composer and his music, creator and creation, are together answerable only to their own act, its purity and integrity; but the performer is answerable to the composer's intention partly embodied in the written score, partly intuited, partly developed as the music begins to live its own life and to reveal its full possibilities. Any piece of music, once it is first uttered, lives within a tradition of interpretation, in which its truth is revealed and lost and discovered again as it is handed down through time by ears and minds and batons which perish and are reborn with it. In each "generation" there are the listeners, the audience, which "must be assured of the merit of the person who presents the work to it and of the conformity of that presentation to the composer's will."[8] Rarely does the music come to full life in the ear and the baton and the instruments of the performers; and composers such as Stravinsky complain of those who sit in "indifference and apathy . . . listening without hearing," while Claude Debussy comments on audiences who listen to his music, their "faces grey with boredom."

The communion of composer and performer and listener in a moment's crafted time is rare indeed, and yet it is the unity towards which the fully self-conscious composer strives. His focused energies fashion a perishing unity in which time coheres and wherein time-ridden creatures and creators may find a moment's coherence and resolution and unity. "Music," says Seu-ma-tsen, "is what unifies." It coheres and in its precarious vortex all that perishes at the same time coheres. For we must "always remember that when [we] listen to a composer's creation [we] are listening to a man, to a particular individual, with his own special personality" and that what the composer conveys is himself, that part of himself "which embodies the fullest and deepest expression of himself as a man and of his experience as a fellow human being."[9] The unity sought in music and rarely achieved is an interpersonal unity, a temporal unity of time-ridden beings, mortal yet enduring, alive, and cohering, and spirited. Of this unity Stravinsky writes:

> For the unity of the work has a resonance all its own. Its echo, caught by our soul, sounds nearer and nearer. Thus the consummated work spreads abroad to be communicated and finally flows back towards its source. The cycle, then, is closed. And that is how music comes to reveal itself as a form of communion with our fellow men—and with the Supreme Being.[10]

But when time draws together into one enduring present and we experience the unity of a sound, a melody, a life—our own or another's, newborn for a first time or from time immemorial—*where* do we stand, *when* are we? We are, it seems, so many doomed gods, half mortal, half immortal, with timeless memories and expectations, and with only timely, deadly prospects. We tell stories, live in them, die in them, and live again as our stories are retold, and die as they are forgotten and the same seems true of our gods.

Although music exists in time and calls man the hearer into the crafted passage of its time, there is a purity in music which eludes and obscures the often fractured, inchoate, irresolute, inconclusive quality of the time of one's life. Melodies or themes come to composers, find their development, and we are allowed to dwell in them to find a moment's coherence. But each time we lose ourselves in a piece of music we must find ourselves again in silence facing the otherwise incoherent moments of our lives. Each person, each self, starts and stops as a matter of course; birth and death go without saying and something will inevitably occur in the in-between. For a fortunate majority of individuals, the full life cycle will take its course, goading on each individual through a gamut of youth, and maturity, and age. Each of the "seven ages" presents its own peculiar tasks and rewards and puzzles. All this goes without saying; and yet a play merely blocked with the most inescapable entrances and exits, a play whose only script is the crying of infants, the sighing of young lovers, and the gasping of the nearly dead—such a drama is indeed "a tale told by an idiot, full of sound and fury, signifying nothing." Men wish for coherence, unity, and resolution not only in their music but also in their lives. Men and women tell stories with their lives. They put together the moments of their lives first with one emphasis and then with another, searching for the rhythm, the theme, the timbre, the harmonic scheme which will bring power and purpose of movement to lives which otherwise fly apart or else lie limp and irrelevant in their own hands. To experience one's life as requiring a melody and a plot is to experience one's life as inherently timeful. And this experience is barred to one who only or primarily sees one's world and one's way through it. One must hear time and listen to the world before reality—one's own and others'—becomes personal (which means soundful) and interpersonal. The visual truth of a common world becomes a shattered illusion as one brings time to mind and reflects on one's death. Clearly I die alone; and thus it would seem that the time of my life never coincides with the time of another's life. We are on a different time; we live separate realities. If I must die alone, then, in all truth, I must live alone, namely, live out the final truth of my life, live consciously towards the resolution which is inescapably mine. This claim for the primacy of death and thus of solitude is central and constitutive for a wisdom or presumptive wisdom which is sometimes called existentialism, a cup of which we in our times have drunk deeply and which has gone to our heads.

And yet this wisdom is flawed by deep inconsistencies and by an inadmissible bias. It assumes the finality of silence, the finality of death, which must always remain quite uncertain, quite fundamentally ambiguous for the isolated individual. One learns of death (or for that matter of life) not from oneself but from others. The certainty of death is something we learn with our eyes and our ears—it is a truth grasped only interpersonally, learned only from others' deaths, only from dying imaginatively with them the very same death. And there is no more dramatic or telling account of this fact than the ancient epic of Gilgamesh, who all but dies with the death of his friend, Enkidu, and then sets out upon a desperate and futile quest of immortality. When asked to explain his pale and frantic look, Gilgamesh tells what he has learned from another's death:

> And why should not my cheeks be starved and my face drawn? Despair is in my heart and my face is the face of one who has made a long journey, it was burned with heat and with cold. Why should I not wander over the pastures in search of the wind? My friend, my younger brother, he who hunted the wild ass of the wilderness and the panther of the plains, my friend, my younger brother who seized and killed the Bull of Heaven and overthrew Humbaba in the cedar forest, my friend who was very dear to me and who endured dangers beside me, Enkidu my brother, whom I loved, the end of mortality has overtaken him. I wept for him

> seven days and nights till the worm fastened on him. Because of my brother I am afraid of death, because of my brother I stray through the wilderness and cannot rest.[11]

And yet if we are to admit the interpersonal, we must admit more than the personal inevitability of death, more than the reality of a common doom. When I look into the eyes of another person and that person looks into my eyes, something very curious takes place. Our eyes remain open, we continue to see; but the visual world is decisively transformed. For what I see, he can never directly see; and what he sees, I can never directly see. We are both see-ers but we cannot share immediately what we see with each other; the objects of our sights may not be visually communed in. And yet we discover a somehow common world. Our eyes meet—but where do they meet? This meeting place belongs more to hearing than to seeing—it is more a time than a place, more clearly a *now* than a here. And yet our eyes do not close, they remain open and fixed, almost without seeing. The world of hearing, we *see*, is not altogether private, not a tunneled world where men hear one anothers' energies and efforts but never meet in them. It is somehow a common world and yet not a world so common that our communing in it calls for the loss, the obscuring, the forgetfulness of our own individuality. To be mindful of this world is to be ever mindful of the times of our lives. It is a realm of experience and of truth to which music introduces us and which comes to fullness of expression in stories. Stories, like music, belong to time and bring always peculiar individual moments, individual lives, into a brief, perishing coherence. And yet they mediate between the uniqueness of my lifetime and the uniqueness of yours; they fill the silence into which your life and my life tip with a sound, a meaning we can follow together. Stories allow us to meet and not simply to pass each other in life. Stories permit us to recognize one another and to linger in the recognition. And most marvelously of all, this recognition permits us to love one another, to accept, to embrace knowingly, what perishes. Without stories we would merely collide, now pleasantly, now painfully, now conveniently, now inconveniently. Atoms would strike atoms but lives would never mingle and converse.

To say that our experience across time is inherently musical is also to say that it is inherently narrative. For we arrange the flow of time into living wholes not only playfully for the sheer joy of its music; but we are desperately concerned to arrange the stream of events in our own lives into acceptably coherent, resolute wholes. There can be no personality, no selfhood, without continuity of time, continuity across time. Unless my life has a beginning and an ending, a plot and a focus, that is to say, unless my life unfolds as music or story, then it is a series of random events, unarranged, out of control, incomprehensible. Here too it seems to be a matter of resolution, of scattered, troubled moments driving towards a moment's repose. And our moments, says Augustine, are our loves, what we seek, what we enjoy, and what we await. In decision, which is finally a matter of love, my life comes together. Even the most insignificant decision, the most trivial love, gathers time together into a moment's focused intensity. The more pervasive and decisive one's love in its implications, the more irreversible and committing in its consequences, then the more cohesive and powerful and spirited one's life becomes in its assertion. The whole purpose of life, says Kierkegaard, is to come to a single decision, to will one thing, and to renew that decision throughout one's life. Resolute, consuming love alone provides identity, purity of heart, and a life lived, he says, *uno tenore*, on a single tone, uttered once forever.

Indeed, it may be that the most perfect musical theme, neither requiring nor permitting variation or development, would be a single tone. Such a tone would be only inwardly, personally meaningful. It would represent more the exclusion of all else than the affirmation of itself. Thus Kierkegaard's urging is that the heart's one will must be negative, the exclusion of all conceivable loves, the creation of a void in which one dwells alone until that void, that silence, erupts into being and voice, namely, until the infinite reveals itself and its will for us. One lives in the desert until the desert blossoms. Augustine speaks of stretching our will, our love, until its restlessness is complete and is unaccepting of, uncommitted to, whatever it encounters. But even if we take pause at such counsel, it seems true that our lives articulate themselves, arrange themselves, around our decisive loves. Our stories are stories of love, their rhythm that of desire and dissatisfaction, of faithfulness and betrayal. Life must be spent if it is to be lived. We direct our lives towards what we desire or what we imagine that we desire. We are what we have loved or endeavored to love. Our life is as coherent as it is resolute, as thematic as it is wholehearted. The eye becomes what it sees and the ear becomes what it pursues, what it follows. The life of man the hearer, the personal life of man, is always a following. Stories are made of followings just as they are made to be followed. Stories—in the telling and in the listening—embody and image our lives in their unfoldings. But what does it mean to follow a story?

To follow a story is to accept a fundamentally humble, servile posture. One must cross over into another time and respond unquestioningly and unhesitatingly to its leadings and windings and pace. To pause, to look back, is to lose one's place, one's footing. Time does not wait, music does not wait, stories do not wait. They are in movement; we are either with them or without them, either for or against them. We cannot move freely, noncommittally, back and forth between several sounds or scores or stories as we might between several perspectives or paintings. Time away from a story is time lost, more or less critical, but always irreversibly lost. To follow a story, then, presumes commitment, acceptance in advance. The storyteller asks or looks to see whether you are listening before he begins and seldom responds graciously to a barrage of midstream questions for further details and explanations which disrupt the pattern and pace and flow of his story. A story is either self-explanatory and self-justifying or it fails. Like a piece of music, a story must compel and persuade one of its coherence and draw one into its purpose and powerful vitality. Teller and listener, like oil and water, are somehow at one in movement until it stops and they begin to settle out again. Following a story is very like following a game of sport. We must know the rules and accept them as at least provisionally interesting and compelling. Children often attempt to alter a game's rules or to create a game all their own; and more often than not they find themselves failing utterly to fashion something they can enter and which will, in turn, take them up into itself absorbingly. The new game or the new rules seem all too arbitrary, too self-consciously complicated, or too simplistic and monotonous. One finds the same to be true of music and of stories. A good story need not be factual, nor decent, nor true to be worth the telling and the listening; nor is fantasy, or ribaldry, or deceit any guarantee of interest. A good story moves and we move with it; and as it develops we are willing to accept all the more eagerly and uncritically whatever it incorporates into its organic rhythm with which we have become sympathetically one. Stories may define the possible and the likely and the appropriate and the necessary so long as they do not violate their own definitions and so long as they do not permit us the freedom and disposition to question them. There is, of course, fair play called for in stories just as in games. The prescribed rules and possible outcomes must, as a matter of course, be adhered to; but the actual outcome should not become too obviously predictable. There are, to be sure, exceptions when we delight in the vandalism of shattered assumptions and expectations or when we delight terribly in the relentless approach of a glaring, hounding fate.

The eye sees at once what is always one in the beginning. The ear hears what is scattered, what simply unravels; and the ear must seek in memory and in anticipation the wholeness and unity of its unfolding. The ear must tolerate tension and dissonance, the illogical, tempestuous, never-the-sameness of time and the timely. The eye strives to discern man, the nature of man, what it means to be man quite apart from what it means to be a child or a woman, or this man in particular. Meanwhile the ear must listen to the endless, fated differences and misunderstandings of persons who happen (not by nature but just happen) to be young or old, man or woman, rich or poor, gentle or rapacious. The eye sees all of these goings-on as shades, as shadows, as fine lines crafted with care and serenity into a visible, reasonable whole as they were by Hephaistos into the spectacle of Achilles' shield. The ear must endure them as ambiguities, contests, strivings, never fully resolved, never less than consuming. When Aristotle discusses the proper form of storytelling, of drama, he thinks of drama as something visible, suited for the theater, the seeing-place. Thus he argues that the plot (*mythos*) "endeavors to keep as far as possible within a single circuit of the sun."[12] In this way, drama more perfectly imitates the beautiful, shapely look of action and life, of happiness and misery. He is centrally concerned with the wholeness and the unity of the plot which he sees as a matter of its proper size and order. Similarly, Socrates reserves a special place, in fact his own last days, for the work of Aesop, who characteristically ends each of his tales with a *logos*, a "moral," to which the story may be reduced and in which its truth may be seen all at once. Each of these primarily visual understandings of story elude the vagaries of sound, of the soundful, the personal, which is dispersed in the medium of time.

Such images spread out like ripples on water when they enter time which is never abidingly present but always either past and thus irreversible or future and thus unpredictable. Man the hearer, the storyteller, takes his stand in the midst of a time, a stream of events, which defies his longing, visionary imaginings of a timeless, simply meaningful present and acts in defiance of time. He denies its denial of his humanity. In the face of an irreversible past, he forgives; and in the face of an unpredictable future, he makes promises.[13] Neither the past nor the future are ruly or controllable; they are rough expanding seas which man must navigate as he will. There is no warrant for forgiveness in what is past and done or left undone; and there is no warrant for promises in an impervious, unformed future. Time is utterly uncontrollable, utterly out of man's hands to shape; man lives at sea's edge and his practicalities are tidal, regularly washed away or left without the salt of life. Man's acceptance of his weakness must encompass his uncontrollable past as well as his uncontrollable future, i.e., must involve the making of promises as well as the acceptance, the forgiveness, of promises made and broken.

Curiously and wondrously, man's action, his promising and his forgiving, creates a story, a present, a shore against the erosive flow of time. This is creation in time raised to its fullest human power. Men tell stories of promises and of forgiveness with their lives as well as with their mouths, stories not only of human fellowship but of fellowship with God as well. For it is from Moses and from the prophets that we learn the full meaning of promise-making and it is from Jesus that we learn the full meaning of forgiveness. Storytelling, we come to realize, is the most utterly serious human business for man the hearer. The stories which concern us most are stories of promise and of forgiveness, stories of fellowships promised and betrayed and renewed rhythmically in endlessly repeating variation and development. These stories are always told on the shore of chaos, they resound in our ears as in abandoned shells; and we are fond of them finally because our God is fond of concealing his own care and power and wisdom in such stories, we are told. These stories seem to tell us as much as we tell them.

> When the great Rabbi Israel Baal Shem-Tov saw misfortune threatening the Jews it was his custom to go into a certain part of the forest to meditate. There he would light a fire, say a special prayer, and the miracle would be accomplished and the misfortune averted. Later, when his disciple, the celebrated Magid of Mezritch, had occasion, for the same reason, to intercede with heaven, he would go to the same place in the forest and say: "Master of the Universe, listen! I do not know how to light the fire, but I am still able to say the prayer," and again the miracle would be accomplished. Still later, Rabbi Moshe-Leib of Sasov, in order to save his people once more, would go into the forest and say: "I do not know how to light the fire, I do not know the prayer, but I know the place and this must be sufficient." It was sufficient and the miracle was accomplished. Then it fell to Rabbi Israel of Rizhyn to overcome misfortune. Sitting in his armchair, his head in his hands, he spoke to God: "I am unable to light the fire and I do not know the prayer; I cannot even find the place in the forest. All I can do is to tell the story, and this must be sufficient." And it was sufficient.
>
> God made man because he loves stories.[14]

The world of this story and this story-loving God is, of course, the world of Hebraeo-Christian thought, the narrative, soundful world of Moses, the prophets, and Jesus. It is a world of good stories and of a wisdom and human fullness which come only from listening to and telling those stories always once again. Clearly there can be no question here of reducing these stories to morals or to principles (*logoi*); finally, like all stories, they must be simply told and followed. Nevertheless, certain possibly rash and sweeping comments may serve to suggest the thoroughly sonorous, musical, and narrative character of biblical experience as well as to complete our own preliminary exploration of the possibility of hearing.

The Hebrew world is prescribedly sightless with respect to God and man; both are wrapped in an interpersonal history of promise and forgiveness which does not admit of visual or pictorial understanding and expression. This Hebrew faith strictly forbids bodily images, either painted or sculpted, of God or of man. When, in later Hellenistic Judaism, such images begin to appear in the synagogues of the Diaspora they still depict primarily active and eventful motifs of faith such as the sacrifice of Isaac, the call of Moses at the burning bush, or the deliverance of the Jews across the Red Sea. And when early graven images are fashioned in violation of this prescription they are mostly dynamic and auditory in significance, describing God's personality and name and not his appearance. To Hebrew experience, the experience of a migratory, desert people for whom the very face of the earth changes with the winds as well as with their wanderings and dislocations, reality is thought of as always in movement, energetic and masterful. It is nonbeing, rather than being, which is motionless and fixed. And their God is appropriately conceived as the consummation and source of all becoming, all effective power. For the Hebrew God all things are not actual but possible (Mark 10:27). God is pure *hayah*, pure becoming, pure effectual power, the power to raise up, to tear down and to raise up again. And it is in the word that this character of God is most perfectly imaged. We must not confuse for a moment, however, the Hebrew understanding of word as *dabhar* with the Greek understanding of word as *logos*. In Greek the beings of thought and speech (*logos*) are, as we have seen, immaterial and never-changing, whereas the Hebrew word is a physical cosmic power, as swift and material and powerful as we can imagine it.

Does not my word burn like fire
—it is Yahweh who speaks—
is it not like a hammer shattering a rock? (Jer. 23:29)

And so when Yahweh—eternal *hayah*, eternal becoming—makes known his presence to men, he comes quite appropriately and characteristically as a word, *the* word which redeems and creates, calls, promises, and forgives. From the first, God is known only through his deeds and his deeds are speeches, words which call forth, fashion, transform, and renew reality. God breaks the silence, the void, which enclouds reality, and there is an inhabitable and inhabited world, illuminated and in all ways provided for. "By the word of Yahweh the heavens were made" (Ps. 33:6). "By the words of the Lord his works come into being and all creation obeys his will" (Ecclus. 72:15). Divine speech creates what may only then be seen rather than disclosing what has always been. The divine word looks to and reveals nothing before or beyond it. The word emerges from and towards nothing. God speaks, his word creates what it signifies, and what now has being is seen to be good. This creation of the word of God is itself wordful. God is speech and what his words create cannot but be alive with speech. All that shares in the reality of God shares in the word. Word is being; and nonbeing is nonword (*lo-dabhar*) or silence. The world in its very being confesses, speaks aloud, the being of its God. The rhythm of creation, even the circuit of the sun, is a mystery not of light so much as of sound to be heard by the soul's ear:

The heavens declare the glory of God
The vault of heaven proclaims his handiwork;
day discourses of it to day
night to night hands on the knowledge.
No utterance at all, no speech,
no sound that anyone can hear;
yet their voice goes out through all the earth,
And their message to the ends of the world. (Ps. 19:1–4)

Man, too, made in the image of God, is one who is born to speak. His nature and the nature of his sovereignty over the creation is left without any account apart from the charge that man is to give things their names. To name something, we should understand with the Israelites, is to fashion it, to control its being and its possibilities. What man calls things, they are, whatever he calls them. Man's imagination has effectual power—he fashions a world for himself with his imaginings and he lives therein. Things are as he regards them to be. But his sovereignty is decisively qualified from the outset. His words, his imaginings are indeed creative but they are not radically, unanswerably creative; for man speaks not over a void but over a creation already called forth and fashioned by divine speech. He speaks over every living thing—things with God-given lives of their own. And so we are not allowed to say simply that man names things and they are whatever he names them, but rather that man names things and they are for *him* whatever he names them. Man, made in God's image, is to rule in his image as well. To rule in someone's image or beneath someone's standard is to rule in the name of another, to rule provisionally as a representative of the actual ruling power. Such a provisional governor has absolute power in the short run, in his immediate dealings and rulings; but he is finally himself answerable. Man's sovereignty is of this sort—decisively qualified and finally answerable. He speaks and creation listens. The first sight of man, says Philo, strikes fear into the hearts of all creatures under man's proper dominion. The beginning of wisdom for such creatures, one might almost say, is the fear of man.

But man too must learn fear. There is no mention or thought of man's naming himself; for himself, he must answer. He too must listen or else his words will violate the will of God already spoken over and ensouled in creation. He must be silent before he speaks and this silence is not his to break and fill. Man as speaker is properly a prophet (from *pro-phēmi*) one who speaks for or on behalf of another. So long as God is silent and so long as creation is silent of God's purpose, man acts "blindly" or, more appropriately, speaks out of turn, as a creator rather than as a creature. To be a man is to speak and yet to speak man must first hear. He is to speak only what he hears. His being, his life, is to embody the word, to give it voice, to sound forth, re-sound, God who is word.

This is the meaning of becoming, of the one, soundful, wordful coming-to-be which binds man and his world and God—all reality—in a dark, per-sonal, complicity.

> From the beginning till now the entire creation, as we know, has been groaning in one great act of giving birth; and not only creation but all of us who possess the first fruits of the Spirit, we too groan inwardly as we wait for our bodies to be set free. (Rom. 8:22–23)

Although the biblical account of Hebrew faith begins with the faithful account of the origins of the world, it is not likely that the creation of the world is the first and central activity attributed to the word of God by Hebrew faith. Rather, the Genesis account of origins seems to complete and to complement the account of Israel's call and deliverance from bondage in Egypt. But it is not urgent that we dispute here the precise relation of possible dependency or derivation between Hebrew creation-faith and redemption-faith. It is enough to realize that the two are finally one faith, one trust and assurance that whatever is or happens is indeed the work of God in which he means us well. God's presence and benevolence are not always evident or manifest, nor visibly confirmed in the form, the shape, of things. Man must look to the heart of things, which is to say that he must see with his heart, blindly, lovingly; for this is the manner of divine sight. "God does not see as man sees; man looks at appearances, but Yahweh, looks at the heart" (1 Sam. 16:7). And if one sees with the heart, sympathetically and faithfully, one sees, one follows, a single story of divine creativity and benevolence, a divine self-bestowal, from the love of creation to the love of its renewal and renewed partnership:

> For now your creator will be your husband,
> his name, Yahweh Sabaoth;
> your redeemer will be the Holy One of Israel
> he is called the God of the whole earth. (Isa. 54:5)

In each decisive moment of Hebrew faith, in each moment of truth, the word of God comes, unexpected and unwarranted, creating its own reality and renewing it, providing its own warrant. Its comings and goings are unknown to man; man is unable to penetrate or to discern the silence from which his God emerges and in which he is awaited any more than he is able to enter the silence, the void, from which creation was first called and from which it continues to be called. Man suffers the events of his world, the rising of the sun, the falling of hail and rain, the bread of heaven, as well as bondage and exile. Man is the plaything of his God; still a beloved plaything. God's ways are not man's ways. To man the slaying of a son is parricide, one of the most hideous of crimes, surely not an expression of fatherhood; and to murder one's son as a child is to lose one's offspring through him. In the more or less measurable and orderly world of moral sight and insight, murder is murder and each act has its consequences to be known and accepted as one acts.

Not so for God. To slay Isaac is to sacrifice and not to murder; and to lose a son is to gain a son with faithful progeny more numerous than the stars of the sky or the sands of the sea. Abraham's faith is accounted righteousness in him—no more is required or conceivable—and becomes a paradigm for the faith of Jews and Christians generation after generation. The faith of Abraham (whose name Philo interprets to mean "the great father of sounds") is a simple trust and a wholehearted residing in the will of God, whose origins and ends, whose motives and purposes, are dark and hidden to him. For the Greeks, truthfulness calls for a laying bare, a disclosing, of what lies dark and hidden (*alēthēs*, truthful, comes from *a-lanthanō*, to bring to light what is concealed); and to act blindly is to act irresponsibly. When Socrates learns of the oracle's saying that he is the wisest of all men, he sets forth to test, to see for himself, whether the oracle speaks truly. For the Greeks, man's calling and his responsibility is to see for himself; what is obscure and unseen lies appropriately in doubt. The Hebrews have no regard, in fact have no word, for doubt. The word of God is not seen to be true; it is true by virtue of the God who speaks or more properly, it is utterly real and powerful and binding. We would say that God speaks with pure authority—a word and a reality unknown to the Greeks—that he speaks and we are to listen. His coming is pure event, pure sound, to which our ears and we as listeners are utterly vulnerable, without recourse, without appeal. To be faithful is simply to listen, to be filled with and to follow the moving, acting, shattering, consuming, enlivening presence of God.

If we reflect upon the clustered meanings of the various derivations of *ȧman*, to be steady and faithful, we may grasp the sense, the spirit, of Hebrew faith: *ȧmen*, verily, surely; *omen*, faithfulness; *ėmeth*, constancy, trustworthiness, certainty; *u̇mnam*, really; *ȯmenah*, pillar, doorpost; *ėmunah*, persevering. One must become as a child for whom words are true by virtue of who utters them; for a child has no experience, no grounds, of his own on which to stand and from which to question. A child's imagination is simply in the hands of his elders, particularly his father, from whom he receives his truths *personally*, soundfully and authoritatively. We may recall young Neoptolemus and his struggle to escape the posture of a child, the posture of one who blindly trusts and does what he is told. And it is not as if Hebrew faith would reprimand him for resisting the authority of the wily Odysseus. For no man speaks with authority—in this certainty Hebrew and Greek wisdom concur—and one is to call no man father but only God. And yet God speaks to men, enters into a fellowship with men inconceivable to the Greeks apart from the Homeric myths in which gods frequently took out their rage and satisfied their passions at man's expense, but surely never cared for men with the enduring constancy of a husband. Hebrew faithfulness is an image of the faithfulness of Yahweh and the childlike simplicity of faith is a response to the fatherhood of Yahweh—his sheer power which leaves one without recourse and his watchful care which leaves one without concern for tomorrow's bread or tonight's shelter. Man is first imaged in Genesis as one who walks in the garden, knowing only the voice of his God, without the knowledge of good and evil, without discernment, and without care. This image remains paradigmatic for the trustfulness and simplicity of the life of the follower, Jewish or Christian, of whom God required "only this, to act justly, to love tenderly and to walk humbly with your God" (Mic. 6:8).

Perhaps nowhere in the Hebrew Bible do divine personality and human personality and their musical, soundful complicity as one who speaks and as one who listens become so resoundingly clear as in the account of the call of Moses. The third and fourth chapters of Exodus present, as it were, an instruction in sound and authority and trust by a God not often so patient and for a servant singularly dear and central to the divine purpose. It is here that God reveals his name to be called upon with faith and assurance by a people beginning to have a voice. God lays himself open, accessible to being invoked, vulnerable to being rejected, when he reveals his name. But we find him already open, already engaged; for he hears the groaning of his people and remembers his covenant with Abraham, Isaac, and Jacob. We are here in the midst of a story, a piece of music, whose plot and theme have already been stated (even if this account is in fact largely constructed in retrospect). God is not free at the sound of his people's lament nor is Moses free at the sound of his God calling him, "Moses, Moses." If this were an Egyptian god's voice or if Moses were not an Israelite, this voice would be without immediate authority. It would have to create fear in the absence of respect by the sheer display of power as Moses will be called upon to bring the Egyptians to their knees with the seven plagues. For the Egyptians do not have ears for Yahweh's words. Even Moses questions God's command to him and asks, "Who am I to go to Pharaoh and bring the sons of Israel out of Egypt?" (Exod. 3:11). *Who* am I to?—the truth, the compelling force of speech is for Moses and for this people a matter of who speaks rather than of what is said. Moses is no one and he expects no one to listen to his words.

This understanding of speech and of what commends one's words to another is, in turn, quite foreign to the Greeks whose assembly assured the freedom of each citizen to speak and sought to guarantee each voice an equally open, equally critical hearing. If anyone attained so preeminent a stature before others that his words began to possess authority, began to be heeded and commended uncritically, such a man required to be ostracized. Ostracism among the Greeks, prior to Hyperbolus the demagogue, was a tribute of sorts, the supreme recognition granted to the personal superiority of one whose person commanded such respect that he jeopardized the free and critical exchange, conflict, and debate of opinions which was seen to provide the best available assurance that the true, the right, course would be laid bare and followed. To Moses, however, God responds that he, Yahweh, shall be at his side and that when Moses speaks, Yahweh speaks. But the people will require to know who you are, to know your name, says Moses, and God tells Moses his name, *Ehyeh-asher-ehyeh* "I will be Who I will be" or "I shall be present howsoever I shall be present" (the renderings of Leo Strauss and Martin Buber, respectively)—sheer self-determination, sheer personal power, freedom, and self-consistency, sincerity. Moses' voice shall be heard even as God's voice—authoritative, unquestionable, and powerful, softening the ears of the faithful, hardening and shattering the ears of the unfaithful. Almost comically Moses questions his personal suitability, who he is to speak when he has an impediment and is quite incapable of eloquence. Moses continues to misunderstand the character of divine speech and divine reality—that like music and story, it needs no warrant beyond itself. And yet God yields to Moses' doubts and allows Moses his own prophet, Aaron. Moses speaks for God and Aaron speaks for Moses who as a god will inspire Aaron. The word of God admits of repetition, variation, and development without loss of force or unity, so long as those who speak for him, his prophets, are not false but true prophets, sympathetic and faithful to his will. But Moses remains the paradigm of the prophet. Only of Moses may it be said that Yahweh knew him face to face, that "Yahweh would speak with Moses face to face as a man speaks with his friend" (Exod. 33:11). Here too we find a striking contrast with Greek understandings. For the Greek the face (*prosōpon*) is something looked upon, while for the Hebrew the face is what is turned toward someone (*panim* from *panah*, to direct, to turn) to meet his eyes and to converse. The one is an object of sight providing appearance and recognition, while the other is an organ for interpersonal meeting and conversation. Moses knew God and God knew him for who they were, intimately, personally.

Face to face with God, Moses does not see God; for "man shall not see me [Yahweh] and live" (Exod. 33:20). Rather, Moses meets eyes with God, not seeing but listening.

God, of course, knew many prophets who spoke his name again and repeated his will that men should walk humbly with their God. The word of God comes to Samuel (1 Sam. 15:10), to Nathan (2 Sam. 7:4), to Elijah (1 Kings 18:1, 31), to Isaiah (2 Kings 20:7; Isa. 38:7), and to Jeremiah (Jer. 36:1; 37:6). Each time the word invades the ear, the life of man the hearer, and finds resonance where it wills. Each time the prophet is left without recourse; for the word of God is simply irresistible. "The Lord Yahweh speaks," says Amos, "Who can refuse to prophesy?" (Amos 3:8). Each prophet calls not himself but is called, speaks not for himself but only what he hears, faithfully and resoundingly. Isaiah speaks for every prophet from Moses to Jesus when he says: "My ears have had this revelation from Yahweh Sabaoth" (Isa. 22:14). And yet as irresistible as the word is for the prophet, for the faithful, there are others who do not hear, a scandal and a mystery.

> Plainly their ears are uncircumcised,
> they cannot listen.
> Plainly the word of Yahweh is for them something contemptible,
> they have no taste for it. (Jer. 6:10)

All faith comes through hearing (Rom. 10:17) but some do not hear, and hearing is a matter of the heart and of love. Some hearts are hardened to God and love other things, always mostly themselves. And so the story of the Lord is one of promise—and like all musicians Yahweh always gives us himself—of faithfulness and mostly of unfaithfulness, and finally of forgiveness and renewal of the promise. All wisdom—all rightness of mind and of heart and of life—begins with fear, with reverence which permits us to listen with our lives, simply and unquestioningly. All wisdom is from the Lord (Ecclus. 1:1), never to be laid bare or disclosed for man once for all. Ben Sira sums up Hebrew wisdom when he counsels: "Listen to me, my son, and learn knowledge, and give your whole mind to my words" (Ecclus. 16:24). When man seeks to see for himself, to discern the natural and the reasonable, he "darkens counsel by words without knowledge" (Job 38:1 RSV). Greek wisdom counsels the man who cannot see his own way to wait or to follow a man of sight, a wise man; and yet Jesus assures us that when one man leads another it is always a matter of the blind leading the blind (Luke 6:34). Aristotle says we are the best judge of others' deeds and the worst judge of our own; for deeds require distanced perspective to be seen. Jesus assures us again that we are to judge not, so as not to be judged (Luke 6:37); for we inevitably notice the speck in another's eye and overlook the beam in our own. The meaning of a deed is hidden in the heart, concealed from others, deep in the intention of its author. We do what we intend to do—to look upon a woman with desire is to have slept with her. Logic forces us to conclude that we do not do what we never intend—to have killed a man by accident is not to have killed him. This is sheer nonsense to the Greeks for whom deeds are primarily public, namely, deeds are more closely equivalent to their shared consequences. And one man, as a rule, when an eyewitness or informed adequately by eyewitnesses, can see quite clearly what another has done. Finally, to Hebrew wisdom, all is dark and unknowable; for all that is and all that happens is from God, the work of God. All time and all history are clay in the potter's hand and only God knows what he has made. "One only is wise, terrible indeed, seated on his throne, the Lord" (Ecclus. 1:8).

"At various times in the past and in various different ways, God spoke to our ancestors through the prophets; but in our own time, the last days, he has spoken to us through his Son, the Son that he has appointed to inherit everything and through whom he made everything there is" (Heb. 1:1–3). This is the ultimate claim of Christian faith—that the word of God has become flesh, that God has spoken not through a human life but in a human life. It is not what Jesus says but who Jesus is that is divine. In him the fellowship, the complicity, the courtship of God and man, of eternity and time, is complete. The labor of creation is come to term in this birth of a child. If he is silenced, the children and the very stones will cry out. As we follow the descent of the word in the "genealogy of Jesus Christ, son of David, son of Abraham," which opens the Gospel of Matthew, we are aware that we are reversing the Platonic ascent from the cave. We retrace our steps into the cave, into the altogether particular, the immediate, the absolutely unique. Here there can be no question of sight and understanding. Here we encounter in altogether blind faith the sheer darkness and obscurity of the divine purpose, the decision for man, to create, to respect, to love. And each man in his uniqueness is called upon to respond, to decide blindly for himself to abandon himself to Jesus, to follow he knows not what where or why into a meaningless death which is the final obscurity.

That the unique individual should concern himself infinitely with another unique individual, that one fated man should contain the meaning of another fated man's life—this is the Christian paradox, mirrored more perfectly in marriage than anywhere else where each person promises to the other to follow they know not where or why, to be faithful to the unfolding of another simply obscure, utterly unpredictable life having no more visible warrant than one's own. The unique is of consummate significance—God cares for, counts, the hairs on one's head—Greek madness and Christian mystery. Jesus says simply "come"; but where and why? He doesn't say. We are to enter his life, to remain contemporaneous with a life lived, a story told and retold. We are never to forget. To promise is to give one's word, to meet eyes, and to know the promise is given and received. In medieval practice, contracts between vassal and lord would be witnessed by young boys who would then be struck a stiff blow after hearing the agreement so as to never forget it. A moment's Pentecost, a moment's confirmation; and one is left with a memory. How does one assure its recollection, its enduring presence? One tells it to children, one tells it to one's sons and daughters, as did God once upon a time, assured that if only the story is remembered it will be enough.

> Rabbi Hiyya said to Rabbi Hanina:
> Is it with me you are disputing, I ,who saved the Torah from being forgotten in Israel?
> What did I do? I went and sowed flax and made nets from it; I caught deer, and gave their flesh to orphans; and I made scrolls from the skins, and I copied the five books of Moses on them,

> Then I went to a town and taught the five books to five children, and instructed the children in the six orders of the Mishnah. And I said to them: Until I come back, study the five books together and instruct each other in the Mishnah. And thus I saved the Torah from being forgotten in Israel.[15]

When Israel stood to receive the Torah,
the Holy One, blessed be he, said to them:
I am giving you my Torah. Bring me good guarantors that you will guard it, and I shall give it to you.
They said: Our fathers are our guarantors.
The Holy One, blessed be he, said to them:
Your fathers are unacceptable to me.
Abraham is unacceptable who said: "Whereby shall I know" (Gen. 15:8).
Isaac is unacceptable to me, because he loved Esau and I hated him, and Jacob is unacceptable who said, "My way is hid from the Lord. " (Isa. 40:27).
Yet bring me good guarantors, and I shall give it to you.
They said to him:
Master of the universe, our prophets are our guarantors.
He said to them:
The prophets are unacceptable to me:
"The rulers transgressed against Me: the prophets also prophesied by Baal" (Jer. 2:8).

Yet bring me good guarantors and I shall give it to you.
They said:
Behold our children are our guarantors.
The Holy One, blessed be he, said:
They are certainly good guarantors.
For their sake I give the Torah to you.[16]

NOTES

1. Sophocles *The Women of Trachis*, trans. Michael Jameson (Chicago: University of Chicago Press, 1957), ll. 693–705.
2. Robert Lowell, "Epigram," in *For the Union Dead* (New York: Noonday, 1972), p. 23.
3. Arthur Schopenhauer, *The World as Will and Representation* (New York: Dover Publications, 1966), 2:28.
4. Ibid., p. 30.

5. Igor Stravinsky, *Poetics of Music* (New York: Vintage, 1947), pp. 37–38.

6. Ibid., p. 128.

7. Ibid., p. 139.

8. Ibid.

9. Aaron Copland, *What to Listen for in Music* (New York: Mentor, 1953), p. 134.

10. Stravinsky, p. 146.

11. Nancy K. Sandars, trans., *The Epic of Gilgamesh* (New York: Penguin, 1971), pp. 98–99.

12. Aristotle *Poetics* 5. 1449b13, in *The Basic Works of Aristotle*, ed. Richard McKeon (New York: Random House, 1941).

13. This discussion of promise-making and forgiveness is largely dependent on and hardly adequate to Hannah Arendt's brilliant discussion of "Action" in part five of *The Human Condition* (Chicago: University of Chicago Press, 1958).

14. Elie Wiesel, *The Gates of the Forest* (New York: Avon Books, 1967), pp. 6–10. The quotation from *The Gates of the Forest* by Elie Wiesel, translated by Frances Frenaye, copyright © 1966 by Holt, Rinehart and Winston, is reprinted by permission of Holt, Rinehart and Winston, Publishers.

15. Nahum Glatzer, ed., *Hammer on the Rock: A Midrash Reader* (New York: Schocken Books, 1962), p. 55. Copyright © 1948, 1962 by Schocken Books, Inc. Reprinted by permission.

16. Ibid., pp. 42–43.

Whoever writes in blood and aphorisms does not wish to be read but to be learned by heart.

Friedrich Nietzsche

CHAPTER SIX

TOUCHING

Hearing—the following of a sound or of a story or of a living, personal truth—is eventful. It comes and it passes, leaving only a memory. And our memories are notoriously selective, often clinging to the merest convenient detail and failing to recall the center. Remembering is not equivalent to hearing, not peculiarly a matter of hearing; for there are memories of sights and smells and feelings as well as of sounds. And they are confused, the one with the other, in the memory of things past, assorted material for our imaginings and for our understandings. Once past, what has been heard is lost to our following ear, it becomes an object of sight and insight, available at once. We inquire into its meaning and its truth. We cannot do otherwise from the distance and the remove of one who lives now no longer within a sound but still within sight of it. So long as one is following a piece of music or narrative, or following the steps of another person, the meaning, the power and the fullness, is personally and presently experienced in the following or not at all. But when we find ourselves again in silence, we must either forget, or wait for the coming of something new or the return of something old, or we must remember, bring to mind, and ask what it all meant, and what relationship might still obtain between ourselves and it, what its enduring truth or meaning or worth might be.

However extraneous and perilous we may regard the art of criticism or interpretation or judgment to be, such is the fate and the calling of one who has listened and wishes not simply to forget but to respond appropriately. In short, sounds, events, (whether music or story or self) once past, become objects of sight, things less well-suited to sight than its own proper objects but leaving no alternative but to be seen and interpreted, or lost. There is no pure rehearsing or retelling; interpretation is simply unavoidable and is thus best lucid and knowing. Plato is indeed proper in calling the love and inspiration, the spiritual possessedness, of the hearer, a kind of heaven-sent madness, bringing not evil but the greatest blessings.[1] And he seems equally proper and persuasive when he says that "God has given the art of divination not to the wisdom, but to the foolishness of man."[2] The wisdom of sight is foolishness to the ear, too remote and uncommitted to enter into fellowship with the truth; and, in turn, the wisdom of hearing is foolishness to the eye, too servile and parochial to be of any shared or lasting significance. And in moments of silence, when sounds are only to be recalled, to be brought to mind rather than to be heard, possessing and overwhelming the mind, the eye is privileged and primary. In times ungifted and unvisited by the gods, in the silent after-moments of sound, it seems right and inescapable that Plato should say:

> No man, when in his wits, attains prophetic truth and inspiration, but when he receives the inspired word, either his intelligence is enthralled in sleep or he is demented by some distemper or possession. And he who would understand what he remembers to have been said, whether in a dream or when he was awake, by the prophetic and inspired nature, or would determine by reason the meaning of the apparitions which he has seen, and what indications they afford to this man or that, of past, present, or future good and evil, must recover first his wits. But, while he continues demented, he cannot judge of the visions which he sees or the words which he utters; the ancient saying is very true—that "only a man who has his wits can act or judge about himself and his own affairs." And for this reason it is customary to appoint interpreters to be judges of the true inspiration. Some persons call them prophets, being blind to the fact that they are only the expositors of dark sayings and visions, and are not to be called prophets at all, but only interpreters of prophecy.[3]

Both the Hebrew and the Greek traditions mostly accept as true that the madness of hearing is brief, that the past is irreversible, and that "only a man who has his wits can act or judge about himself and his own affairs." Both faiths have their privileged interpreters and interpretations. These are their truest sons, their guarantors, to whom the sacred stories are retold and abandoned. For children belong not nearly so much to the past as to the future. They dream dreams of their own, tell their own stories with the stories given them. They debate with one another and with the future; and the truth is handed over to and in their debates. One hopes they have their wits about them and that they have once listened faithfully and remembered well as children before they have ideas and stories and lives of their own. "In the matter of religion," says Kierkegaard, "it is a very serious fact that one learns the best things as a child." For a moment one is contemporaneous with the word, with every believer who ever walked humbly with his God, and in the next moment one is left to concur or to oppose what the elders, what most men with their wits about them, what those named to speak for the others, have made of what they've heard. Henceforth it is a matter of opinion (*doxa*) of right opinion and wrong opinion, claims to orthodoxy, and arguments on behalf of such claims.

Lest Plato's remarks be thought foreign to the experience of faith, which they are not, we may listen to much the same wisdom spoken from within Hebrew faith and recorded in the Mishnah.

> On that day Rabbi Eliezer brought all the proofs in the world, and the masters would not accept them.
> He said to them—If the law is according to me, let this locust tree prove it.
> The locust tree moved a hundred cubits. (And some say: four hundred cubits.)
> They said to him—The locust tree cannot prove anything.
> Then he said to them—If the law is according to me, let this stream of water prove it.
> The stream of water turned and flowed backward.
> They said to him—The stream cannot prove anything.
> Then he said to them—If the law is according to me, let the walls of the House of Study prove it.
> The walls of the House of Study began to topple.
> Rabbi Joshua reprimanded them:
> If scholars are disputing with one another about the law, what business is it of yours?
> They did not fall down out of respect for Rabbi Joshua, and

did not straighten up out of respect for Rabbi Eliezer,
and they are still inclined.
Then he said to them—If the law is according to me, let
the heaven prove it.
A voice came forth from heaven and said—
Why do you dispute with Rabbi Eliezer?
The law is according to him in every case.
Rabbi Joshua rose to his feet and said—
"It is not in heaven" (Deut. 30:12).
What is the meaning of—"It is not in heaven?"
Rabbi Jeremiah said:
The Torah has already been given once and for all from
Mount Sinai:
We do not listen to the voices from heaven.
For You have already written in the Torah on Mount Sinai—
"After the majority must one incline" (Exod. 23:2)

Rabbi Nathan came upon Elijah.
He said to him: What was the Holy One, blessed be he,
doing at that moment?
Elijah said to him:
He was smiling and saying—My children have defeated me,
my children have defeated me![4]

The word is not in heaven—the word was given once for all—we no longer listen to voices from heaven but to each other—no man speaks with authority—only a man with his wits about him is a proper judge. If we put all of these scattered claims together, we must, it would seem, conclude to the simple primacy of the eye in the lives of men, mostly uninspired and unvisited by the gods. Yet the rivalry of eye and ear, of the spiritual possibilities of "free insight" and "obedient love," is an endemic struggle which seems to permit no lasting truce, no final resolution amenable to each. No one in our times has more lucidly and honestly pursued this dilemma than the late Leo Strauss who places the two—seeing and hearing—at clear odds, where he finds them to be, when he writes—

> Man cannot live without light, guidance, knowledge; only through knowledge of the good can he find the good that he needs. The fundamental question, therefore, is whether men can acquire that knowledge of the good without which they cannot guide their

> lives individually or collectively by the unaided efforts of their natural powers, or whether they are dependent for that knowledge on Divine Revelation. No alternative is more fundamental than this—human guidance or divine guidance. The first possibility is characteristic of philosophy or science in the original sense of the term, the second is presented in the Bible. The dilemma cannot be evaded by any harmonization or synthesis. For both philosophy and the Bible proclaim something as the one thing needful, as the only thing that ultimately counts, and the one thing needful proclaimed by the Bible is the opposite of that proclaimed by philosophy—a life of obedient love versus a life of free insight. In every attempt at harmonization, in every synthesis however impressive, one of the two opposed elements is sacrificed, more or less subtly but in any event surely, to the other—philosophy, which means to be the queen, must be made the handmaid of revelation or vice-versa.[5]

I have cited this passage by Strauss at length because it represents a brilliantly insightful and honest assessment of the dispute between faith and reason which has hounded Western religious thought and particularly its three great religions—Judaism, Christianity, and Islam—from their origins and continuously ever since. He lays bare the quite distinct roots of each opposing experience and claim and suggests the impossibility of their resolution. And this intransigence in Strauss's formulation finds ample precedent in such early thinkers as Tertullian who asks rhetorically:

> What has Athens to do with Jerusalem? What has the academy to do with the church, and heretics with Christians? Our instruction issues from the porch of Solomon, from whom we have learned that the lord is to be sought in simplicity of heart. . . . We have no need of curiosity now that we have Jesus Christ; nor any need of inquiry, now that we have the scripture. Our believing leaves nothing beyond it to be desired.[6]

This same irreconcilable disparity, even hostility, between the way of believing and the way of understanding represents not only the experience of believers from within their faith but represents as well the perception of nonbelievers from within their lives of honest questioning and thinking. In fact it is the first thing noticed by Galen, the second-century Roman philosopher and physician, who is among, and perhaps the center of, the first pagan intellectuals in the Roman world to notice and to remark on the phenomenon of Christianity. It was then, during the reign of Commodus, that Christianity invaded for the first time the higher circles of Roman society after years of mutual distrust and contempt. Contrasting sharply the study of medicine with the study of Hebrew and Christian truth, Galen remarks, "If I had in mind people who taught their pupils in the same way as the followers of Moses and Christ teach theirs—for they order them to accept everything on faith—I should not have given you a definition."[7] Celsus, Galen's contemporary, remarks more harshly of the Christians that "they are like quacks who warn men against the doctor, 'Take care that none of you touches science (*epistēmē*), science is a bad thing, knowledge (*gnōsis*) makes men decline from health of soul.' "[8] And the emperor Julian, addressing Christian believers, sums up the character of Christian arguments when he says: "Yours are want of reason and rusticity, and all your wisdom can be summed up in the imperative 'Believe.' "[9] Finally, there is no more unyielding and eloquent delineation of free insight and obedient love than Søren Kierkegaard's essay, "The Difference between a Genius and an Apostle," which I can do little more than mention. It may suffice to note here that what is both crucial and representative about Kierkegaard's discussion of this dilemma is his singling out of *authority* as the simply decisive issue. The conflict between believing and understanding, as it has developed in religious thought, was and is an issue of distinct and conflicting human possibilities, human postures or "ways" towards reality rather than of specific claims regarding reality. That is, the dispute was not primarily over *what* one knows or believes but over whether one *knows* or whether one *believes*.

Even so, despite the perhaps inevitable authority of Rome with its pronounced bias for faith as for practical concerns and solutions, briefly and splendidly, Athens and Jerusalem mingled and conversed and filled to overflowing the souls of thinkers such as the Hebrew Philo and the Christian Clement and Augustine. For a moment both possibilities coexisted in a turbulent, exciting dialogue, in a pattern of beautiful contradictions. And yet this coexistence, the speculative fullness of the words of Philo and Augustine, is beyond the scope of our present considerations. They share the assumption of all philosophical theologians, i.e., that what they believe is true; and in doing so they assume the posture of the philosopher, the primacy of seeing, of inquiry and speculation. They suggest the possible unity of what can be known and what can be believed but leave unresolved the disputing multiplicity of truth as pursuit, as human posture and possibility. They represent the dialogue of two possibilities, a dialogue without practical, without possible, outcome. It is Rome, and the possibility of authority, which discloses still another possibility and which fashions the image of man from which we must immediately take our bearings. It was the Rome of Caesar and not of Augustine, nor, for that matter, of Virgil, that prevailed and shaped modern Western experience.

In his discussion of Christian belief, Saint Augustine often distinguishes the faith which believes (*fides qua*), the act of faith, from the faith which is believed (*fides quae*), the content of faith. And it is the act of faith, faith as act rather than as creed, which is central and decisive from the beginning and increasingly so. It may be argued that the Western, i.e., the Roman, theological tradition was always marked and eventually dominated by essentially practical rather than speculative concerns. Liturgy, the daily life and organization of the Christian community, preoccupied the Roman mind and appealed to Roman genius; and it was Rome which emerged as the unrivaled heir and successor to both Athens and Jerusalem.

The Roman people, if I may venture several sweeping and somewhat disparaging statements, were a supremely practical people with barely their share of imagination. Their advances, mostly military, were solid and careful and effective, but rarely adventurous or romantic. They were mostly a people of whom an empire rather than a literature would likely emerge. And they were proud rather than deferring with respect to their eminent practicality which so well suited them for what came to be their calling, the protection and preservation of the genius and the apostle, Greek wisdom and Hebrew-Christian faith. Tacitus, one of Rome's greatest historians, says that all their energies and plans should serve the practical necessities of life, should be directed *ad utilitatem vitae.* And the elder Cato speaks of the ideal Roman as *vir fortis et strenuus*—a man of strong courage and enduring energy. It was said of the Romans that they never went to battle but always to war, namely, that their spirit and purpose could not be broken by a single or by several defeats. Regardless of their many blunders and defeats, defeat was what they refused to recognize, and they seemed to learn, to gain in prudence and resolve, from their failures. A people of farmers, they were rooted in a rugged determination, a posture of constant struggle against what resists cultivation and taming, and a confidence in the renewal and final fruitfulness of their energies. Thus they turned defeats into victories, and drove on to total conquest and systematic rule. Their ambitions were practical, modestly low-minded and yet indefinitely expansionist. The Romans fought neither for spoil nor for glory but for security. Neither luxurious nor vain, they were, as Virgil describes them:

> a race from sturdy stock.
> For first we bear our infants to the river
> and harden them by cruel frost and water;
> and then our boys grow keen in hunting, ranging
> the forests; and their sports are breaking horses
> and aiming arrows from their bows. As youths
> they learn frugality and patient labor
> and tame the earth with harrows or compel
> defiant towns to tremble.[10]

Or so they fancied themselves, and indeed proved to be. Their myths and legends, fewer and less grandiose than the Greeks, tell mostly of heroic deeds and, particularly, of the founding of cities. The Romans were fond of describing their own shared character with several qualities which together sketch for us their ruggedly earth-ridden image of man: *pietas, gravitas, continentia, industria, diligentia, constantia, virtus.* The Roman, fitted to withstand centuries of unremitting life-and-death struggle, was of necessity loyal and dedicated, serious and steadfast, self-contained and dependably hardworking, schooled and practiced in endurance, courageous, and staunchly reliable. These are practical, rather low-minded qualities which, however, admit of accomplishments of unparalleled scale and scope. If one follows their path from Africa to Asia Minor to France to Britain, one follows a path of strict utility and yet of staggering expansiveness. Their arches and walls and fortresses are solid and imposing and everywhere. The traces they have left of themselves tell of a people who knew and sought and achieved above all else not the beautiful or the good or the faithful, but the powerful. Their wisdom, neither that of contemplation nor of utter trust, is a wisdom solidly practical, what the Greeks called *technē* (whence our technology) and what we call know-how. They were familiar with storm and pressure and assault of every sort, skilled in resisting and in exercising force; neither greedy nor vindictive, they were utterly serious in their pursuit of power, which they wielded fairly and with relatively little flourish. They saw their power as god-given, entrusting them with a god-given work which Virgil summarizes for them and describes for us who wish to know how they conceived of their proper *ergon* or work:

> For other peoples will, I do not doubt,
> still cast their bronze to breathe with softer features,
> or draw out of the marble living lines,
> plead causes better, trace the ways of heaven
> with wands and tell the rising constellations;
> but yours will be the rulership of nations,
> remember, Roman, these will be your arts:
> to teach the ways of peace to those you conquer,
> to spare defeated peoples, tame the proud.[11]

The culture, the *paideia*, of the Romans was largely derivative. They mostly imitated, copied, and preserved the art and philosophy and literature of Greece. Their own souls were too without leisure, too preoccupied with the urgent and the perilous, to live speculative or creative lives of their own. (Perhaps the one wondrous exception to these and other rather extreme assessments of Roman low-mindedness is the *Aeneid* of Virgil from which I occasionally draw for images of Roman character and to which I nowhere do justice.) Their genius took a more immediate practical turn: the arts of discipline, law, and government, not the political philosophy of Plato and Aristotle, but closer, instead, to what we might call military or political science. For Plato and Aristotle, knowledge of the good is what entitles and suits one for rule; and for the Hebrews leadership is a matter of divine call and designation. The Romans, however, prefer cunning and hand-to-hand skill, the experience of military campaigns, as qualifications for rule, together with near-absolute power. What we find here is a practical convergence of authority and power. A fortress people cannot survive and cohere, cannot respond to the urgencies and necessities of its existence, without deeply rooted discipline and duty. Obedience to authority is a theme, a habit or bent of spirit, which veins Roman life, private and public, the life of the family and the life of the state. The head of the family had unquestioned authority over all members of the family; and the king, correspondingly, had unquestioned authority over all members of the state. In the family this authoritative power is called *potestas* and in the state *imperium*. Roman *imperium*, once conferred upon a king by the human members of the state, by an act of the people, and once sanctioned by the divine members of the state, by the obtaining of favorable omens (*auspicia*), is simply irresistible. This *imperium* is a threefold power representing supremacy in religious, legal, and military affairs. Although the king's power was absolute, he was normally governed by custom in the exercise of his power regarding religious and legal matters. The priests (*pontifices*) and diviners (*augures*), counseled him in the former and a council of elderly men (*senatores*) advised him in the latter. It was in the field, with the army, that the king's power was unqualifiedly absolute. A Roman king at war was beyond the realm of his own deities and unsworn to the local deities. He was beyond custom, answerable to no one. And it was this power, the altogether arbitrary power of the warlord, the pure fusion of authority and force, which crossed over from war to peace, from the exception to the rule, from field to city with Caesar and began to give shape and legitimacy to a third human possibility, the possibility of touching, of moving and of being moved, of causing and of mastering the movements of things and of peoples.

We have called Roman culture derivative. In fact, the Romans contribute little else (again I must except the *Aeneid*) to Greek genius and Hebrew-Christian faith than their preservation, which was no trivial feat, and which the Greeks and Jews were ill-suited and ill-situated to provide for themselves. The cost of this asylum, however, was a discipline and a systematization rather foreign to the simple beholding of the loveliest things and to walking humbly with one's God. Partly it was a matter of codification and copying and defending texts. More deeply, however, it was a matter of translation into a peculiarly Roman institution—*traditio*. Rome inherited Greek and Hebrew-Christian wisdom, often in curious odd and exciting confusions and gathered them together, assembled them in "the gathering" (*ecclesia*), the church. This assembly is Roman in origin, as are the tradition and authority which support its foundations and pillars. The word "authority" (*auctoritas*), for which there is no precedent in Greek or Hebrew understanding, comes from *augere*, which means to extend, to perpetuate, to "augment." And what is continuously and primarily augmented in every aspect of Roman life is the act of founding, that most sacred of acts, in which, as nowhere else, human and divine activity become one. "For there is really no other occupation," writes Cicero, "in which human virtue approaches more closely the august function of the gods than that of founding new States or preserving those already in existence."[12] And, of course, that preeminent act of founding which bestowed upon the Roman people and their gods a new home was the founding of the eternal city of Rome brought to fullness of conception and commemoration in the *Aeneid* of Virgil, who sums up the travail and pain of that founding in the famous lines: *"tanta molis erat Romanum condere gentem"* (so great was the burden of founding the Roman people). The most thoroughly Roman divinities were Janus, the god of beginning, and Minerva, the goddess of remembrance. The Roman people and state were bound to the soil, to a specific locality, circumscribed by the sacred plow, the furrow dug by Romulus and consecrated to gods of hearth and house, as were neither the wandering Jew nor the Greeks who could take to their ships and remain a polis.

The Romans were deeply religious and religion was a matter of being bound, tied, held back (*religatus*), relegated to the past and eternal act of founding, to the past of the city ensouled in its custom and laws. In short, no race had a more conservative character than the Romans. Roman fathers announced the birth of sons with the saying *auctus sum filio* (I am extended in, carried on or augmented by a son); and this was precisely the central and comprehensive calling of the Roman to augment, to extend, preserve, and hand on the work, the life, of their elders, the *patres*, those who in collaboration with the gods once laid the foundation of all things to come, the founders, the *auctores imperii Romani conditoresque*. And it is surely apparent how closely the Roman Catholic Church, the *ecclesia*, patterns itself after this ideal of organization and conservation. The Roman church takes its origins from its founding upon the rock, the slow, precarious, finally steadfast faith of Peter and the quite thoroughly Roman structure which emerged in his name.

It is critical to Roman and to Catholic understanding that the decisive act, the sacred commerce of the gods and men, be regarded as an accomplished fact of the past, namely, that the word of God be once and forever spoken, abiding now on earth, no longer coming down from heaven. The Scriptures become a canon of Scripture and the claim of faith is no longer that God speaks to men with authority but that God has spoken to men with authority. The act of revelation, the reality of divine presence and activity, is seen as an act of founding, an act of enabling. The basis for the *ecclesia* is not so much either the Christian faith in the resurrected Christ or the Hebrew reliance upon the word of God but rather the events of Jesus' life and death recorded in the Scriptures and unfolded in the church year, the liturgical cycle of the *ecclesia* which exists and lives for the commemoration of those events. The Roman church is reluctant to be drawn into speculative or purely theoretical debates. Only hesitantly does it define dogma and heresy which it does only to preserve its established way of life and thought, its custom, and never spontaneously to clarify truths which remain obscure or hidden. The transcendent power and reality and incomprehensible fullness of being, of Yahweh, and of the kingdom announced by Jesus have become tamed and taming household gods, supporting, authorizing, and enabling a proud people to live as they have lived and to civilize others into the same modest patterns.

This may seem unduly harsh and narrowly obscurantist, failing in due recognition of the monks and the reformers and the pentecostals and the philosophers of Rome. My overlooking them, however, is a matter of Rome's overlooking them, too intent, too grave, and constant, and eventually corrupt for their rash excesses. Rome exorcised Greek and Hebrew-Christian madness, the divine madness of the philosopher and the prophet, with the finest of intentions and unavoidably. The word had been spoken and pure hearing was no longer possible; and the sunny, learned, otherworldliness of the Greeks had fallen upon dark and urgent times. The very possibilities of hearing and of seeing seem to be obscured and all but removed by the silence of God and the direful, dark moments when necessity reigns. Hearing and seeing become possibilities of the past, legacies, treasures to be recorded and preserved. *Paideia*, education, is no longer the rearing into sight or into hearing—men learn not to see or to hear but only the fact that men once saw and what they saw and the fact that men once heard and what they heard. Tradition is wisdom in the past tense; and the present is now given over to the development and the legitimation of a new possibility, a possibility we know only too well—the possibility of touching.

Greek wisdom and Hebrew wisdom are, in fact, preserved in a peculiarly derived and confused state in Roman wisdom. We find traces of them everywhere, but they cease to be distinct, fully understood and embraced possibilities. They lose their integrity, their power, and their radical, consuming vitality. They become private and idiosyncratic—studies, predilections, or professions. It is quite conceivable and convenient that one should become a philosophical skeptic, an orthodox priest, and a ruthlessly pragmatic politico, all at once. Eventually, in Europe, at the beginning of the modern era, the very possibility of seeing and the very possibility of hearing were relentlessly and systematically denied and thought to be refuted. In fact they were merely ridiculed and the ridicule held because all that remains of these possibilities were ridiculous remnants—the Scholasticism of the schools and the bloodied, fractured, decadent *ecclesia* which Luther, with earlier prophetic precedent, likened to a whore. What is significant is that it is institutions that are rejected, or rather a single institution which was rejected, the Aristotelian church. It is not Rome that is rejected; for Rome's institutionalization of Greek and Hebrew-Christian possibilities is approved in their being rejected as unacceptably institutionalized. And Rome itself is approved, not the Rome of Virgil or Peter or Augustine, but the Rome of Caesar.

The Rome of Caesar is at its center altogether secular, surprisingly so. Rome remained basely pragmatic and tolerant in its pursuits, singularly unconcerned with the contending claims of Athens and Jerusalem regarding the one thing needful, the one all-encompassing, all-consuming good, the *summum bonum*. The good which Rome pursued was collective rather than common, a fundamentally dark, obscure, ambiguous good-power. But its designs upon and for power were modest, relatively benign, and conservative—the securing and the preservation of a decent way of life—human fate made no worse than it need be and perhaps slightly bettered. They were driven by no vision or following of the one thing needful; rather, they were indifferent to *the good* but appreciative of the goods available to the powerfully cautious and persistent. Mostly they were driven by the dread of an incessantly threatened existence; the endless claims of necessity and peril distracted and determined them upon a course of constant war against a world which would not allow them their modest hopes and their fill. In all of this they have become our fathers. Even their religion fails to bind them, to tie them back, and stands only to serve their modest and yet imperialist dream of security from the uncontrollable. In doing so it betrays its fundamental secularity, its utter subservience to man's designs and energies. It is mostly the plaything of men and thus men become utterly serious and grave and responsible for themselves and for their fate, a purely human thing in man's hands. Religion finally does no more than show up the frail efforts of men to found lasting towers and assurances in the sand, to found the cities of man on earth which Augustine saw as a succession of foundings, of powerful assertions unable to sustain themselves.

It is appropriate that Cicero should present us with a sceptical Roman priest as the spokesman for Roman religion in his *De natura deorum*, a priest who frankly has no idea what man can expect from the gods or even less what the gods might expect from men. His arguments for religion are instructively pragmatic. Without belief in the gods and their care for men, there would be no piety, without piety no religion, and "when these are gone, life soon becomes a welter of disorder and confusion; and in all probability the disappearance of piety towards the gods will entail the disappearance of loyalty and social union among men as well, and of justice itself, the queen of all the virtues."[13] Cotta is a priest and, while others are caught up in the endless debate of one equally tenable opinion against another, and regardless of his own personal opinions, he is reminded of his commission to augment, to preserve, the tradition of the founding of the city of Rome. He agrees to go on with the discussion so long as any such discussion is understood in advance to be of no final bearing.

> Very well [he says], let us then proceed as the argument itself may lead us. But before we come to the subject, let me say a few words about myself. . . . I am both Cotta and a pontiff. . . . I ought to uphold the beliefs about the immortal gods which have come down to us from our ancestors, and the rites and ceremonies and duties of religion. For my part I always shall uphold them and always have done so, and no eloquence of anybody, learned or unlearned, shall ever dislodge me from the belief as to the worship of the immortal gods which I have inherited from our forefathers.[14]

Cotta's faith is blind. He listens and does not see. But he listens to human voices which speak with authority. What can this mean to say that man speaks with authority? To respond to this question we must consider the possibility which Rome prepares for and suggests to us and which finds its fullest expression in our innermost image of man and of human possibility—the possibility of touching.

There was no doubt a time when touching, feeling, represented a breakthrough, a marvelous watershed in the evolution of organism; and there was indeed a sense of exhilaration at the dawn of the modern age when the sense and spirit of touch was liberated and legitimized and explored with a single-mindedness more or less new to it. Nevertheless, our usual access to touch is through deprivation, through the removal of all sights and sounds, through our own removal into a sightless, soundless world. I have indeed carried on such experiments with my own students, experiments with blindfolds and ear plugs of various sorts and effectiveness; and it has been to my amazement how suddenly and thoroughly the reality of touch, of a soundless, sightless, yet impinging world, closes in upon one, presses against one. These experiments were initially prompted by my conviction, hardly novel or terribly venturesome, indeed a commonplace, that modern wisdom from Machiavelli and Descartes to Heidegger is constructed upon the twin denial of Athens and of Jerusalem, namely, of seeing and of hearing. Its own assertions emerged from its central and constitutive denials: (1) there is no true sight, all sight is projection or illusion; (2) there is no truly authoritative speech, no man speaks with divine authority and the gods do not and never did speak to men.

If one is, then, in search of the most elemental, the simplest experimental roots of characteristically modern (continental) thought, and of our shared modern character, one need only darken one's eyes and seal off one's ears, denying the possibilities of seeing and of hearing, to discover anew the deepest, darkest, most primitive possibility available to man—the possibility of touch. From the first we notice that touch, our touch, relies upon and resembles and recalls seeing and hearing, which are now, in Rome, only remembered possibilities. And, of course, it is always impossible to isolate fully one dimension of sense and spirit from the others. Modern thought is ghosted by, is unthinkable and unintelligible apart from, ancient thought. But we shall do our best to forget as did our modern forbears, and to imagine, to sense and to think of, ourselves as touching a merely touchable world. Descartes says that all thought must begin by doubting, in principle and radically, all previous opinion; and John Constable, the modern British painter, once said, "When I sit down to make a sketch of nature the first thing I try to do is to forget that I have ever seen a picture." This willed forgetfulness, the willful denial of the tradition, of the possibilities handed down by Rome, the possibilities of seeing and of hearing, pervades and constitutes modern wisdom which is a wisdom of denial and revolt. However, we are the more knowing and lucid moderns if we notice how thoroughly and defiantly preoccupied is modern thought with its losses and its denials. One who despises and denies anything or anyone is still consumed and determined by what he is breaking from. Exhilaration, loss, self-righteousness, and self-doubt are the burden of the rebel and they scar us all. We have never been at peace with our denials; and for good reason.

The world of touch is a world of pressure and force. We touch, we feel, only what presses against us and what we press against. Objects, forces, enter our space and we enter theirs. Either they give way or we give way. We test their texture, their extent, their mass against our own. It is a world of opposites and contraries, tangibly so. Quite simply, it is the world of cause and effect, of moving and of being moved, of causing and of being caused. Causality is admittedly an inference to visual perception or sight; and it is the observation of so-called causes and effects, of billiard balls to be exact, which would lead Hume to claim that "causation" is not given in sense perception. To the passive, distanced sense of sight causation is not immediately given and requires to be inferred from what is given. True enough, and Kant accepts this negative conclusion of Hume's. However, not all sensation is distanced and passive. Touch requires neither the habit of association nor the structuring of a higher consciousness to experience causation directly. Touch is active as well as passive, a matter of moving as well as of being moved. In the experience of moving objects, of feeling them move under the pressure of our directed force, move where and as we move them, we perceive ourselves directly as cause, as agent. This is the central discovery and assertion of the world of touch—the discovery and assertion of ourselves as agents, as causes, as effective forces, as determinately powerful.

Here in the possibility of touch is the perfect fusion of wisdom and power which Plato saw as the precondition for the just *polis*, for the cessation of evils in the city, and which Bacon heralded as a great instauration sure to issue in an infinity of inventions and devices lightening, even transforming, the burden of human fate. Or so it would seem. Unfortunately this instauration is decisively qualified in several respects. The wisdom which is so well-suited and akin to the power of causation is finally merely instrumental, a blend of cunning and know-how. And man's power, his resourcefulness, so apparently unlimited and benevolent, is fraught with ambiguity and threatened by utter despoilment. Power carries with it no assurance of goodwill. Indeed, if there is any discernible relationship between power and virtue it would seem to be inverse in its proportions. And this is as true of our perception of God as it is of our perception of man. Only the weak and battered Jesus saves the image of God from the harshest of readings. And the increase of power seems to carry with it the increase of weakness. Our activities are our passivities and our passivities are our activities. We suffer what we do and do what we suffer. Man's control, his mastery, is limited in its grasp as are his hands with which he touches and moves and shapes. What man sets into motion and fashions into being is soon beyond his control; it becomes a mass, a force, foreign and inherently disloyal to him. This was the lesson which Rome learned—that as it extended the borders of its power and its control it extended the borders of its vulnerability. It became utterly weak, slow, and helpless as it grew in magnitude and power. For man, mastery and slavery are inseparable, interchangeable, indistinguishable. One recalls the common-sense Greek discussions of diet and health and exercise, of human nature and proportion, and wonders what we have forgotten and why.

If we raise the possibility of touching to its highest power of lucidity and self-consciousness we arrive at the constitutive, the founding myth of our times, the myth of the state of nature, a myth of founding. Like all myths it offers an imaginative rather than a literal account of our origins and designs. If we reflect upon it with care, we find in it a sure likeness, a clear echo of our common soul, our second nature, schooled in Faustian ambition and haunted with the darkest, most devil-sent fears, we grasp ourselves as at once pure tyrants and pure victims. The myth of the state of nature imagines us into being as causes and effects in a world of touch. Several times in my classes I have set several students loose, their eyes and ears covered, groping and grasping their way and then, after several hours, read to them this imaginative account of the experience of the state of nature. The fit is tight and terrifying.

> There are, beyond me, beyond the borders of the skin, other things, earth, air, fire, water, living things. I walk on otherness, breathe it, am warmed or burned by it, thirst for and drink it, hunger and devour it. I am, in short, full of desire, driven by desire, never able to consume the whole, to merge all the objects of my desire with myself so as to end the gap between me and other. There is no end to my desire in time except I end. No end to my desire in space; everything, even what is most repellent today, may be tomorrow what I ache for.
>
> But, if I hunger, I also fear. All the other things have their ways, their motions, powers, crushing weights, their sharpnesses, suckings, smotherings, burnings, blastings that may devour me, submerge me, snuff me out in their own processes. But I have wits both to escape those other things and trick them, as it were, turn them to my purposes as they, witless, crunch on—my servants. But however sharp my wit, I am weak before their terrifying force, before their horror-striking, gorgon-headed multiplicity, before their swift and silent stealth. And my hungers give me too little time to lay my stratagems and find out sure retreats.
>
> Worse still, there are others like me: driven by desires as inexorable and as various as mine. If I could enslave them, we could turn our collective wit and strength to do my sweetest willings. But see how they think the same! Flee! But if I stumble and he does not? Fight! The odds are only 50–50. Hide! At nightfall he will sleep and can be killed at better odds. But if he wakens? And will he not try the same thing? And will the others not have a thought like his and mine tomorrow? Or perhaps they think it now and someone will spear me through the back tonight as I bend over the body of my enemy whose sleep has been turned to death.
>
> If we could but agree to some fair sharing of burden and booty we could marshall our collective forces to guarantee the pact and to launch a war of conquest against remaining otherness, against nature, subdue her, break her open and each can take his share of her to his private place, alone, and have his private ways with her, alone, and do his private things with her, alone, in accordance as his desire turns, alone, secure in having her for when and as he wants her. And our being together in the pact and in our common

> army ensures that she never frees herself again to make us fear her once again or that, when, on rare occasion, she floods and shakes loose her chains, we can tie her up again quickly and each return to such delights as he alone knows best. And when, perchance, our desires match we can invite one another into our castles and share the expense of the music, and share the use of one another's bodies, as we dance together, alone, touching, alone, moving as one in our chosen rhythm of the moment, alone, our mutual harmony of motion agreed upon as fair, contracted for, each with each, paid for, each by each, alone; a terminable contract, one gets tired of everything, and, as the next thing, perhaps that will be alike for us, perhaps not, no one can say that for another, each must say it for himself, alone, and only death can end that loneliness in ending each, alone.
>
> The virtue of justice is the keeping of that fair pact whereby each is guaranteed his safe little sphere of loneliness.[15]

This myth describes an existence threatened by and threatening everything which lies beyond its borders. This image of threat and counterthreat, force and counterforce, is reminiscent both of the Romans' obsession with their own beseiged borders as well as of the incessant sufferings and probings of our own sense of touch. I would suggest that there is kinship here of images and experiences seemingly so distant and diverse.

There can be no question now of focusing on one aspect or spokesman of modern thought after another to find the ambition and the terror, the power and the weakness, the mastery and the servitude of this myth developed in full. As we approach the ground immediately before us and at our feet, the pace at which our thoughts have all along been moving becomes simply dizzying. Rather, we must find still another metaphor, a governing image by which to glimpse, to hear, to touch ourselves one last time in recognition. The image which I have in mind belongs to the world of touch and yet shows the peculiarly diminished forms of seeing and hearing upon which touch relies. The image I have in mind is that of man the craftsman, the demiurge, the would-be shaper and mover and master of things.

The craftsman's eye looks within for form and without for material and projects the one upon the other. He looks at a forest and sees lumber for his houses. He looks at the torrent of a river and sees the power to drive his machines. The world outside him has no reality, no worth or meaning, other than that which the inner life of the craftsman, its needs and designs, shed upon it. The other, the nonself, whatever is not one with the willing subject, is over against it as material, raw and resistant, to be subdued and given form and purpose. This posture of man to his world, the posture of the craftsman towards material and towards his work is not peculiar to modern Western man. Men have always known craft, have always constructed, reconstructed the world into, objects to serve their purposes and better meet their needs. Men have always built tools, and shelters, and so on, when they needed them. Artfulness, craft, what the Greeks called *poiēsis*, is not a recent or Western discovery. What is peculiar to us, however, is that we have come to see *poiēsis*, the exercise of our own kinetic power, production, as the properly human work (*ergon*) in which we achieve full stature and being, and, what is more, that we see the world, the whole, the other, the nonself, as the proper object of our own production. In religious language we see ourselves as gods. In political language we see ourselves as tyrants. In more amenable, pedestrian, practical terms we see ourselves as problem-solvers.

The most perfect and the simplest formulation of what I mean by a "problem" is the modern algebraic equation, say, $3x = 9$. To solve this equation is to discover the value of x, the unknown. One may go about this randomly; but such a problem admits of a systematic, methodological solution which is largely the point, after all. But can we say that x is unknown? It is surely given in and defined by the other terms. It is not yet explicit, not yet actual, in some sense; but it is given and rigidly determined. Its meaning is controlled, limited, possessed from the beginning. Now for a quite bold claim—that algebraic, methodological understanding serves as the normative pattern for all characteristically modern studies and understandings. Just as in $3x = 9$ there is no genuine unknown, no searching beyond but only within what is already somehow, circumspectly known, so all characteristically modern research seeks within the known what assuredly is within one's powers to comprehend and control, what admits of pure and simple ideas and definitions.

Francis Bacon remarked that "the human intellect left to its own course is not to be trusted . . . the universe to the eye of the human understanding is framed like a labyrinth; presenting as it does on every side so many ambiguities of way, such deceitful resemblances of objects and signs, natures so irregular in their lives, and so knotted and entangled."[16] It is the measured sketch of the craftsman, the controlled experiment of the scientist, i.e., a fixed method which, in the manner of a prism, refracts the random chaotic light into predictable and surely functional patterns. Human understanding is properly violent and cunningly purposeful in its energies. Thus Kant claims: "Accidental observations, made in obedience to no previously thought-out plan, can never be made to yield a necessary law, which alone reason is concerned to discover. Reason . . . must approach nature in order to be taught by it. It must not, however, do so in the character of a pupil who listens to everything that the teacher chooses to say, but of an appointed judge who compels the witnesses to answer the questions which he has himself formulated."[17] The "Copernician revolution," in the broadest sense, is hardly limited to the observations of astronomy. Rather, it figuratively represents a comprehensive despair of the naked eye and denial of the visible world available to the naked eye; correspondingly, it represents a despair of common sense, or simple reflection upon common prephilosophical experience, and a denial of the intelligible, visibly ordered, whole available to such reflection. Instruments or methods, (particularly the ground lens, the telescope and the microscope) designed to allow and to structure experience according to a preconceived plan, constitute modern man's rapport with his world. His posture is that of a craftsman and we may appropriately recall the words of Francis Bacon when he writes: "In behalf of the business which is in hand I entreat men to believe that it is not an opinion to be held, but a work to be done."[18] And this work, the fruit of learning, is not ancient wisdom but "the invention of an infinity of devices to enable us to enjoy the fruits of agriculture and all the wealth of the earth without labor, but even more so in conserving health, the principle good and the basis of all other goods in this life."[19] This vision, eminently modest and practical, is recognizably Roman and, in retrospect, naïve.

The original criticism leveled at ancient wisdom by Machiavelli and others was that it aimed too high and fell too low, namely, that it aimed at what was beyond man's power to realize and so overlooked what was within man's power to realize. It overlooked the most fundamental of distinctions between the controllable and the uncontrollable, the moveable and the immoveable. It is in touch that we learn intimately the ways of movement and change so scorned by the Greeks and so divinized by the Hebrews. Thus Francis Bacon calls ancient wisdom the wisdom of boys not yet able to propagate, impotent and playful, and irresponsible. True enough, childhood, lasting, lifelong childhood in its utter trust and simplicity, in its endless stream of questions and wonderings which so break adult, purposeful stride—childhood was an ideal, though differently understood, for Greek and Hebrew alike. Not so for a world and a wisdom come of age. And yet we may recall Augustine's remark that adult work is every bit as much playfully trivial and futile as child's play without the joy and delight that comes with recognizing it as such. Yes, ancient wisdom aimed high, too high for man's powers of sure accomplishment, at what could only be a pure gift, at virtue in the fullest sense of that word. And yet the alternative to this endless, humble questioning and striving does not seem to be a benevolent dictatorship over man and nature but bald tyranny. Man, it seems, is made to transcend himself either in the direction of the divine or in the direction of the bestial. Man lives on the edge of his own reality led beyond himself by the Platonic king, half man and half god, or led beneath himself by the Machiavellian prince, half man and half beast. No being is more precarious, more finely balanced than man's. It seems to him he might soon take flight or fall forever. Angel, devil, serpent and bird—all are images of man in his many metamorphoses and possibilities. Camus, in *The Rebel*, brings us moderns to full consciousness when he shows how we have retold the myth of Prometheus and transformed it into the myth of Caesar, the image of blind, benevolent power. It is a parable for our times.

> Here ends Prometheus' surprising itinerary. Proclaiming his hatred of the gods and his love of mankind, he turns away from Zeus with scorn and approaches mortal men in order to lead them in an assault against the heavens. But men are weak and cowardly; they must be organized. They love pleasure and immediate happiness; they must be taught to refuse, in order to grow up, immediate rewards. Thus Prometheus, in his turn, becomes a master who first teaches and then commands. Men doubt that they can safely attack the city of light and are even uncertain whether the city exists. They must be saved from themselves. The hero then tells them that he, and he alone, knows the city. Those who doubt his word will be thrown into the desert, chained to a rock, offered to the vultures. The others will march henceforth in darkness, behind the pensive and solitary master. Prometheus alone has become god and reigns over the solitude of men. But from Zeus he has gained only cruelty; he is no longer Prometheus, he is Caesar.[20]

The modern dream is finally one of tyranny, altogether forgetful of the shared wisdom of both sight and hearing—that man is finally the plaything of the gods. Nothing new. Once the dream of Thrasymachus, the dream of simply invisible, utterly unaccountable power. The dream of Caesar; and of Hobbes, for whom freedom meant simply the absence of all obstacles, the elimination of all impediments to one's movement. Tyranny is surely one of man's great imaginings, one of his most universal "possibilities," consuming and compelling in its truth, which fills the heart of Eteocles when he says:

> I'll speak to you, Mother, without concealment:
> I'd go to the stars beyond the eastern sky
> or under the earth, if I could do one thing,
> seize tyranny, the greatest of the gods.
> I will not choose to give this good thing up
> to any other, rather than keep it myself . . .
> So on with fire, on with swords of war,
> Harness the horses, fill the plain with chariots,
> knowing that I will never yield this rule.
> If one must do a wrong, it's best to do it
> pursuing power—otherwise, let's have virtue.[21]

This dream of powerful tyranny is nothing new, nothing surprising. Where we stand on new ground, however, is in our taming of this dream, our sharing it the one with the other, namely, in our collective tyranny. This is the meaning of the social contract—a would-be end to fire and swords and chariots, a final truce in the war of all against all, a fair share of the booty and the plunder for everyone, each in his own assured sphere of loneliness a would-be tyrant, the world, the whole, existing for, responding to, his every whim. Of course, one's whims will require disciplining and sorting; one's sights must be appropriately lowered. But in the end we are assured loneliness, the removal of impediments, the absence of push and shove, not only silence and darkness but motionlessness. As we approach this zero point, this sensual and spiritual entropy, so awesomely dramatized in Becket's *Endgame*, we might recall the last stage of Creon, who wished to answer to no one and found himself ruling a desert beautifully, alone. We are told by Heidegger that this desertedness, the abandoned solitude of the self, brings the call of conscience, and the summons of the self to its ownmost possibilities; but we are reminded too of the prophet Jeremiah's saying of the false prophets that "they speak a vision of their own heart" (Jer. 23:16). The tyrant, the false prophet, the would-be craftsman of the universe, the modest urbane citizen who wishes only that for once his world might do as it is told and go his moderate way, they all are not nearly so godless as they imagine. Such men, and we among them, in our darkest most selfish moments fashion an appropriate god to whom we are utterly vulnerable and answerable, a god given body by our machines, our leviathans, and our own comfortably isolated lives, a god reminiscent of Polyphemus, the cyclops—one-eyed, savage, and inhospitable:

> . . . You will recall at first his titan strength and Lording spirit, which I trust are to the mark. However, I find his single eye to be his decisive qualification for this post. You see, despite one's strength, with only one eye there is no way of distinguishing what is within ready reach from what is far beyond one's grasp. And one who is so poor a judge of distance will do no better with size. He will never know the scale of his deeds or of others', nor will he ever know whether what confronts him is within his powers or simply overpowering. He will pour his most desperate energies into the slightest endeavors and think to walk away effortlessly with the weightiest matters. In his great size and hapless might he

will resemble the awkward youth whose own misplaced feet are often his greatest stumbling blocks. As such there will be something winning about his impetuous ways but something terrible as well. He will not be easy to live with.[22]

NOTES

1. Cf. Plato *Phaedrus* 244–45.
2. Plato *Timaeus* 71e, trans. Benjamin Jowett, in *Plato: The Collected Dialogues*, ed. Edith Hamilton and Huntington Cairns, Bollingen Series, No. 71 (New York: Pantheon Books, 1961).
3. Ibid., 71e–72b.
4. Nahum Glatzer, ed., *Hammer on the Rock: A Midrash Reader* (New York: Schocken Books, 1962), pp. 96–97. Copyright © 1948, 1962 by Schocken Books, Inc. Reprinted by permission.
5. Leo Strauss, *Natural Right and History* (Chicago: University of Chicago Press, 1953), pp. 74–75.
6. Tertulliani *De praescriptione haereticorum* 7. 33–40 (*Corpus Scriptorum Ecclesiasficorum Latinorum*, vol. 70 [1948]).
7. See R. Walzer, *Galen on Jews and Christians* (New York: Oxford University Press, 1949), p. 15.
8. Ibid., p. 53.
9. Ibid., p. 55.
10. Virgil *Aeneid* 9. 607ff., trans. Allen Mandelbaum (New York: Bantam Books, 1972), pp. 234–35.
11. Ibid., 6. 847–53, pp. 160–61.
12. Cicero *De re publica* 1. 7 trans. C. W. Keyes; Loeb Classical Library, vol. 213 (Cambridge Mass.: Harvard University Press, 1966).
13. Cicero *De natura deorum* 1. 2 trans. H. Rackham; Loeb Classical Library, vol. 19 (Cambridge, Mass.: Harvard University Press, 1967).
14. Ibid., 3. 1–2.
15. Cf. E. A. Goerner, "Reflections on the State of Nature," as yet unpublished lecture given under the auspices of the "Hampshire College Lectures in Philosophy of Religion," Spring 1973.
16. Francis Bacon, *The Great Instauration*, in *The Works of Francis Bacon, trans.* James Spedding et al. (London: Longmann & Co., 1870), pp. 17–18.
17. Immanuel Kant, *Critique of Pure Reason*, trans. Norman Kemp Smith (New York: St. Martin's Press, 1965), p. 20.
18. Bacon, p. 21.
19. René Descartes, *Discourse on Method*, 6. 62, in René Descartes, *Philosophical Essays*, trans. Laurence J. Lafleur (Indianapolis: Bobbs-

Merrill Co., 1964). Copyright © 1964 by The Bobbs-Merrill Company, Inc. Reprinted by permission of the publisher.

20. Albert Camus, *The Rebel*, trans. Anthony Bower (New York: Vintage, 1956), pp. 244–45.

21. Euripides *The Phoenician Women*, trans. Michael Jameson (Chicago: University of Chicago Press, 1957), ll. 503–8, 521–25.

22. Taken from a speech of Socrates in an unpublished dialogue entitled *Phidias* which the author wrote for production at Hampshire College.

The beasts and the birds have memory, or else they could never find their dens or their nests or all the other things their way of life needs; indeed without memory they would be unable to have a way of life. So I must pass beyond memory to come to Him who separated me from the four-footed beasts and made me wiser than the birds of the air.

Saint Augustine

EPILOGUE

REMEMBERING

Most authors, I suspect, occasionally fear that they will be utterly misunderstood, not only in their finest distinctions but even in their boldest, most central assertions. And I must confess that I share this fear of being found dull and pointless, drenched and shivering in the ink I once hoped to spread out so meaningfully. I know that I now find myself wishing for the assurance of one wholly lucid and sympathetic reading, one review, as it were, which would lay bare and repeat with unmistakable clarity what I have most wanted to convey. I suspect that many other teachers will recognize in themselves the same devil-sent doubts and the same awkward tenacity to what requires to be handed on and illuminated; and we must beg the understanding and pleasure of others in this. Leaving nothing here to chance, I wish to attach to my own reflections a parable and commentary by Vladimir Solovyev which offer me the assurance which I seek. These words of the great Russian philosopher and prophet Solovyiev drive with sheer beauty and power to the very center of my convictions and aspirations in writing this book. My own efforts at thinking and speaking truthfully are directly illumined and most demandingly judged by the vision and the ring, and the touch of his simple story. In reading it I wonder what I might have thought to add.

We are fossiled beings, the very veins which feed our flesh and soul bear the spirit of the remote past. Our future and our past are tangled; and we live in that tangle as in a net. "A man's character is his destiny," writes Heraclitus who also assures us that "reality likes to hide." our future is concealed in our past and our past is little known to us. We are mostly inexperienced, living from day to day. Would to the gods that it were otherwise. Which is rather the way Socrates parts ways with Phaedrus after a trek and a conversation not unlike this one in its concerns. He invokes the gods, whichever are present and appropriate, and prays that he might live in full accord with his possibilities of sense and of spirit, both at one and not at war with each other. And they go on, as we might, to end as follows: "*Socrates*: Is there anything more we can ask for, Phaedrus? The prayer contents me. *Phaedrus*: Make it a prayer for me too since friends have all things in common. *Socrates*: Let us be going"[1]—with friendly feelings, I might add, and with a fair tale for the sake of a moment's entertainment and recollection, one last and lasting moment in common.

Do you know this fairy tale?

A huntsman lost his way in a dense forest; tired out, he sat down on a stone beside a wide, raging stream. He sat there looking into the dark depths and listening to the woodpecker tapping and tapping against the bark of the tree. His heart grew heavy within him. "I am as lonely in life as I am in the forest," he thought. "I have long lost my way, wandering by different paths, and there is no way out for me. Solitude, misery and perdition! Why was I born, why did I come into this forest? What good to me are all those birds and beasts that I have killed?"

At that moment someone touched him on the shoulder. He saw a bent old woman, such as generally appear on such occasions—thin as thin can be, and her skin the colour of a locust pod or of an unpolished boot. Her eyes were sullen, two tufts of grey hair stuck out on her chin, and she was clothed in precious robes that had turned into tatters, through age.

"Listen, my good man, there is a place on the other side that is a regular paradise! Once you get there, you'll forget all your troubles. You'll never find your way to it yourself, but I'll take you straight to it—I come from those parts myself. Only, carry me across the stream, for I could not struggle against the current. As it is, I can hardly stand on my feet and am almost at my last gasp—and yet I don't at all want to die, not at all."

The huntsman was a good-natured young man. He did not in

the least believe the old woman's words about the place like paradise, it was not in the least tempting to wade across the stream, and not at all alluring to carry the old creature on his shoulders, but as he looked at her, she had a bout of coughing and shook all over. "I can't let an ancient creature like her perish!" he thought. "She must be over a hundred years old and have borne a lot in her day, so it's only fair to do something for her."

"Very well, granny, climb onto my back, and mind you pull your bones together, for if you fall to pieces there will be no picking them up in the water."

The old woman climbed on to his shoulders and he felt a weight as heavy as if he had lifted a coffin with a corpse in it—he could scarcely move. "Well," he thought, "it would be a shame to turn back now." He stepped into the water, and suddenly the weight seemed less, and then it grew lighter and lighter with every step. And he felt that something miraculous was taking place. But he went straight on, looking in front of him. When he stepped ashore, he looked back: instead of the old woman an enchanting maiden, a real queen of beauty, was clinging to him! She brought him to her motherland, and never again has he complained of loneliness, or killed birds and beasts or lost his way in the forest.

Everyone knows some version of this fairy tale, and I too knew it as a child, but only today I felt its real meaning. The modern man hunting after the fleeting momentary goods and elusive fancies has lost his right path in life. The dark and turbulent stream of life is before him. Time like a woodpecker mercilessly registers the moments that have been lost. Misery and solitude, and afterwards—darkness and perdition. But behind him stands the sacred antiquity of tradition—oh, in what an unattractive form! Well, what of it? Let him only think of what he owes to her; let him with an inner heartfelt impulse *revere* her greyness, *pity* her infirmities, feel *ashamed* of rejecting her because of her appearance. Instead of idly looking out for phantom-like fairies beyond the clouds, let him undertake the labour of carrying this sacred burden across the real stream of history. This is the only way out of his wanderings—the only, because any other would be insufficient, unkind, impious: he could not let the ancient creature perish!

The modern man does not believe in the fairy tale, he does not believe that the decrepit old woman will be transformed into a queen of beauty. But if he does not believe it, so much the better! Why believe in the future reward when what is required is to deserve it by the present effort and self-denying heroism? Those who do not believe in the future of the old and the sacred, must at any rate remember its past. Why should he not carry her across out of reverence for her antiquity, out of pity for her decay, out of shame for being ungrateful? Blessed are the believers: while still standing on this shore they already see through the wrinkles of old age the brilliance of incorruptible beauty. But unbelievers in the future transformation have the advantage of *unexpected joy*. Both the believers and the unbelievers have the same task: to go forward, taking upon their shoulders the whole weight of antiquity.

If you, the modern man, want to be a man of the future, forget not in the smoking ruins your father Anchises and the native gods. They needed a pious hero to transfer them to Italy, but they alone could give him and his descendants both Italy and power over the world. And that which we hold as holy is mightier than the Trojan gods, and we have to carry it further than Italy or the whole of the earthly world. *He who saves shall be saved.* That is the secret of progress—there is not and there can be no other![2]

NOTES

1. Plato *Phaedrus* 279c, trans. R. Hackforth in *Plato: The Collected Dialogues,* ed. Edith Hamilton and Huntington Cairns, Bollingen Series no. 71 (New York: Pantheon Books, 1961).

2. Vladimir Solovyev, *An Anthology*, ed. S. L. Frank and trans. Natalie Duddington (London: SCM Press, 1950), pp. 224–26.